Dogs' Most Wanted™

The Top 10 Book of Historic Hounds, Professional Pooches, and Canine Oddities

Alexandra Powe Allred

Brassey's, Inc.

WASHINGTON, D.C.

Library of Congress Cataloging-in-Publication Data

Powe-Allred, Alexandra, 1965–
    Dogs' most wanted : the top 10 book of historic
hounds, professional pooches, and canine oddities /
Alexandra Powe Allred.
        p. cm.
    Includes bibliographical references (p.) and index.
    ISBN 1-57488-801-3 (pbk. : alk. paper)
    1. Dogs. 2. Dogs—Miscellanea. 3. Dog breeds. I.
Title.

SF426.P68 2004
636.7—dc22   2004008332

Printed in Canada on acid-free
paper that meets the American National Standards
Institute Z39-48 Standard.

Brassey's, Inc.
22841 Quicksilver Drive
Dulles, Virginia 20166

First Edition

10   9   8   7   6   5   4   3   2   1

Contents

List of Photographs

Preface

Most of the remains of the paradomesticated dogs found by archeologists have been dated to about twelve thousand years ago. Some are dated even earlier, but what is interesting about the twelve-thousand-year-old sites is not only the locations—North America (Beaverhead Mountains in Idaho and Utah), Europe, Asia, and pre-Columbian America—but also the similarities in the ways early dogs lived. It appears that humans and dogs lived together harmoniously from the beginning. They lived, ate, slept, hunted, and fought together—one helping the other to survive.

This early bond between humans and dogs set the precedent for their future relationship. Throughout the course of history, we have been side by side. In times of war and in times of peace, the dog has been a faithful companion. Countless lives were saved in World War I, World War II, Korea, Vietnam, Desert Storm, and the Second Gulf War by the brave acts of trained dogs—often sacrificing their own lives. Countless hearts have been healed by the undying love and affection of faithful pets.

It is astonishing how often we have mistreated and abused this historical relationship with dogs, yet they always seem to forgive us. Even though we have abandoned, abused, and destroyed them, they have not turned against us. Always, our friend the dog is there for us, anxious to be with us, eager to please.

History is filled with love and hate, wars over religion and property, good versus evil. One constant in our lives has been the dog—always vigilant, always faithful, always willing, always giving. There is no better example than the images of the Oklahoma City bombing. In 1994, when American terrorists blew up a federal building in Oklahoma, hundreds of people were injured, killed, and/or missing in the demolished building. Rescue dogs were called in to locate bodies (dead or, it was hoped, alive) in the rubble. The pads on their feet were ripped up from twisted metal and shattered glass and scalded from still-burning rubble. Yet, handler after handler reported how the dogs wanted to go back in and search more—always in the hopes of finding a survivor. This wasn't something the dogs did for rewards or their dinner. Finding victims was all these heroic pups could think of. But too often, all they were able to find were the deceased and for many of these brave rescuers, the pain was unbearable. Reportedly, the dogs became depressed and discouraged. Periodically, trainers would hide a person—a volunteer—to "be rescued" to lift the spirits of their canine friends and give them the strength to carry on.

This is how much they love us. This is how giving and caring they are. This is how magnificent and grand their character is. Through the course of time, they have become stronger, truer friends to humans. So, while this book is intended to provide fun facts for the dog lover, it is also a reminder to all of us just how amazing the canine is and why the relationship between humans and dogs must always be cherished.

This book is dedicated to the dogs who have lived to save us from ourselves, who have loved us despite ourselves, and have often died doing no less.

I
History of the Dog

Top Dog Myths of Our Time

In medieval times, a howling dog was considered to be an omen of misfortune or even death. If a dog howled just as a baby was born, it was believed that the child would have bad luck for the rest of his life or, worse, that the child would be susceptible to evil. On the other hand, a black and white dog that crossed a pedestrian's path ensured good business ventures, and it was once believed that Fairy Dogs could lead a lost person to safety. Throughout history, humans have had a tumultuous relationship with dogs—we have loved them, feared them, despised them, and worshipped them. From this relationship some of the greatest legends and myths have been born. Some still persist today.

1. WHY DOGS WATCH US EAT

We believe our dogs watch us eat because they are patiently waiting, full of hope that we will give them a few scraps. Actually, this is a passive/aggressive behavior in the canine world. The dog is trying to stare us down so that he might have his turn eating. This is one reason animal behaviorists and trainers suggest not having dogs in the room while you eat.[1]

2. A YEAR IN THE LIFE OF A DOG

As long as anyone can remember, it's been said that every year of a dog's life is equal to seven years in a human's life. While this may be a rough approximation, it is a mistake to try to compare humans and dogs in terms of aging. At the age of 10 months, many dogs can become impregnated. While that is young even by canine standards, we don't accept the notion that human girls could be pregnant at less than seven years. According to the American Animal Hospital Association, even different breeds of dogs mature differently. Smaller breeds may live as long as 18 years, whereas a large breed like the Great Dane averages only six years.

3. A DOG'S MOUTH IS CLEANER THAN A HUMAN'S

Little kids share lollipops with their puppies, and some people even let their dogs lick an open wound because we've always heard that a dog's mouth is cleaner than a human's. Although it is true that humans have all kinds of germs, and we carry more bacteria than dogs, the germs, like ages, are different. As the American Animal Hospital Association points out, dogs consume things such as raw meat, feces, and bile, which humans would not and could not. "Clean" may be a matter of opinion.

4. "MY VET SAYS I SHOULD LET MY DOG GO THROUGH ONE HEAT . . ."

Canine experts used to say if you let your female dog go through one heat (breeding season), she will be a more confident, calm animal. Actually, there is no evidence of this. Instead, there is now documentation of the downside of allowing a female to go through a season. The stress of keeping her and her living area clean, keeping unwanted suitors away, and the fact that early spaying (at ten weeks) can prolong a dog's life provide strong arguments for having your female dog spayed as early as possible. Spaying is a preventive against uterine and ovarian cancer as well as a practical way of preventing the deaths of millions of unwanted puppies every year.

5. NEUTERING OR SPAYING YOUR DOG WILL MAKE HIM OR HER FAT

The American Animal Hospital Association is clear on this point, as are animal behaviorists: too much food and a lack of exercise and discipline are the most direct causes of overweight dogs. There is no evidence of spayed/neutered animals gaining weight as a result of the procedure. Just as there is a national epidemic of obesity among Americans, the problem is also growing in the canine world. As owners are becoming more and more sedentary, so, too, are their four-legged friends.

6. WHY DOGS EAT GRASS

Everyone knows that when a dog eats grass he has a tummy ache, right? Actually, dogs eat grass for two reasons. The first is boredom. Why not? If they are outside all day without toys or entertainment, gnawing on grass might not seem like such a bad idea. It might also be a diet deficiency. Many dog foods contain too much meat. By tracing the diet of the first known dogs, animal behaviorist Dr. Ian Dunbar contends that we are denying our dogs the veggies and fresh grains they need and desire; that lack of variety may encourage grass-eating.

7. THE BRAIN OF A DOBERMAN

This is a personal favorite of many Dobie owners. Urban legend has it that Doberman owners should be very careful because the brain of a Doberman pinscher does not stop growing, causing great pain and pressure against the dog's skull. For this reason, they can become very violent, erratic, and even deadly. "Absolutely untrue," says veterinarian Jim Rook. The rumor began because Dobies are considered highly intelligent despite their sleek, narrowly shaped head. "It's an urban legend, nothing more," says Rook.

8. DRY, HOT NOSE

When in doubt, feel your dog's nose. It's long been held that if your dog has a warm, dry nose, this is a clear sign that he doesn't feel well. In truth, a warm, dry-nosed pup can be a very happy and content puppy. The real indicator of a sick puppy is frantic panting, glassy eyes, and a high fever—which is measured rectally. A dog with a temperature of more than 102.5 degrees is considered feverish.

9. BREWER'S YEAST AND OIL REMEDIES

Home remedies to fight skin problems and fleas often call for brewer's yeast and/or edible oil. According to the American Animal Hospital Association, most skin problems are caused by food allergies, fleas, or poor diet. Your vet may also prescribe additional oils and fatty acids that may be added to your dog's food. As for treating fleas with brewer's yeast, there is no evidence that it acts as a deterrent.

10. BARKING DOGS DON'T BITE

If a dog is barking, he can't bite you, right? The idea is that a barking dog is merely talking, and it's all bluster. In truth, a barking dog guarding his territory needs to be respected and taken very seriously. The expression, "Let sleeping dogs lie," carries the same message: If you don't know the dog, leave him alone.

The Beginning of the Dog

Just when dogs walked into the lives of humans (and why) is a subject of long debate among dog lovers and animal historians. Are they descendants of wolves? How did they first come in contact with humans, and how were early dogs used? Before these questions can be answered, it is important to trace the prehistoric evolution of the dog.

How the Prehistoric Canine Evolved in Ten Categories

1. *Cynodictis* appeared approximately forty to sixty million years ago, followed by
2. *Pseudocynodictis*
3. *Hesperocyon*
4. *Tomarctus*
5. *Carnivora canidae* or "*lanis*"

Canis EVENTUALLY EVOLVED INTO THE ANIMALS WE RECOGNIZE TODAY, WHICH BROKE INTO DIFFERENT BRANCHES:

1. *Canis aureus* (jackal)
2. *Canis vulpes* (tree foxes)
3. *Canis latrans* (coyotes)
4. *Canis lupus* (wolf)
5. *Canis familiaris*[1]

Today's dogs (*Canis familiaris*) are the domesticated descendants of the wolf (*Canis lupus*). From the *Canis familiaris*, modern-day (that is, within the past five hundred years) breeding practices have enhanced specific features or qualities most useful to humans. It is from breeding practices that we have developed our hounds, herding breeds, and so forth. But what scientists have most wanted to know is how and when the wolf became our "best friend."

1. THE FOREFATHER OF DOGS

About fifty million years ago, in the Eocene epoch, miacis was the forefather of all *canids* (as well as more distantly related carnivores). The miacis was a small, weasel-like animal with a well-developed brain, equally adept at living on the ground and in the trees. By the Miocene epoch, more than forty-two different kinds of doglike *canids* had emerged, the beginning of the modern canine.

2. BRONZE AGE IDENTIFIES FIVE GROUPS

Fossil remains estimated to be some 6,500 years old have identified the five *Canis* groups, signifying crossbreeding and new development of species in the *Canis* family. The wide variety of breeds we see today came from selective breeding and natural genetic mutations in the *Canis* groups.

3. DOGS AND THE GENETIC CLOCK

A study led by biologist Robert K. Wayne of the University of California at Los Angeles argues that canines have been part of the human "family" far longer than previously believed. The study claims that dogs were domesticated one hundred thousand or more years ago, only thirty thousand years after the first sign of modern human beings. The genetic mutations discovered provide more than just information about the crossbreeding habits of the early *Canis*; they also serve as a "genetic clock" that gives a more accurate time line in the evolution of the dog.[2]

4. ANCESTRY OF THE DOG TRACED BACK FIFTEEN THOUSAND YEARS

Archeologists have found a fourteen thousand-year-old jawbone in Germany and twelve thousand-year-old canine bones in Israel. The greatest genetic variation among dogs has been discovered in East Asia, suggesting that as the location where dogs first diversified into a variety of "breeds" with different physical characteristics.

5. AMERICAN DOGS

Many scientists believe that early Asian dogs migrated to North America and bred with existing wolves, thus beginning genetic changes. The ancestors of the Carolina Dog, believed to be from the Bering Strait, were probably brought to North America by Asians some eight thousand years ago. Unlike the migrating

Asian dogs, wolves did not migrate to South America; they were brought by early traders.

Traders from China introduced the Chihuahua to Mexico, likely the oldest known breed in the Americas. The influence from the Orient is clear in the development of dogs in the Western Hemisphere.

6. OLDEST KNOWN BREED

The pharaoh hound is the oldest recorded breed. Inscriptions of the pharaoh hound have been found in the tombs of Egyptian pharaohs and in ancient artwork. This breed was probably a descendant of the Phoenician hound, traded throughout the Mediterranean. The pharoah hound is thought to have been a companion dog, but it was also an excellent hunter—swift and powerful. Remarkably, these characteristics are still appreciated today, and the hound is used for hunting rabbits or feathered game.

7. LOST AND FOUND: THE BASENJI

Like the pharaoh hound, inscriptions of the basenji have been found in the tombs of Egyptian pharaohs and in five thousand-year-old wall drawings. Though this is one of the oldest known breeds, it has remained more or less as it was from the beginning. Unfortunately, like the Afghan hound, many of its roots have been lost. For the basenji, early art will have to tell its history. In modern times, it has been called the Congo Dog of Africa and was introduced into Europe in the early 1930s.

8. THE RISE OF SHEEPDOGS

As early as the Stone Age, mastiff-like dogs were used to fight and protect property. As humans began to use and rely on dogs more and more, the dog's role of protector broadened to include livestock. Food, skins, transportation, and/or income relied heavily on the safety of livestock. As nomadic shepherds in Asia continued to use the dogs throughout the centuries, Phoenician merchants carried them to Europe, where the dogs bred with local canines, creating new variations of sheepdogs. One important change was in color. Early herdsmen preferred their dogs to be white, making them easier to distinguish from a bear or wolf as the shepherds ran to the rescue—club swinging. The Asian dogs that bred with European dogs of many colors lost their distinctive all-white coats.

9. GONE WILD

Although history shows the gradual domestication and breed clarification of the dog, not all cases have been successful. More than four thousand years ago, the dingo was brought to Australia as a domesticated dog. Much as the dogs of the post-Roman Empire were left to fend for themselves, so, too, was the dingo. Now a feral dog—that is, a once domesticated animal that has reverted back to the wild—the dingo has become a problem animal for the people of Australia.

10. DOGS TODAY

At one time, only families of great wealth or nobility could have dogs. Today, worldwide, more than two hundred million dogs are kept as pets. In North America alone, the largest dog-owning nation, more than sixty million dogs are household pets. French and Russian households each have more than ten million pet dogs, and pet owners in Japan and Britain have approximately seven million dogs as companions.[3]

Famous Canines
in History

The emergence of the domesticated dog changed the course of history. How wars were fought, armies were fed, kingdoms were run, and societies prevailed are linked to our interaction with dogs. Science, medicine, and literature all have been profoundly impacted by our four-legged friends. From the beginnings of the domesticated dog to human's first step into space, dogs have earned themselves a place in history.

1. THE DOGS OF ALEXANDER THE GREAT

Ancient legend has it that an Illyrian king gave Alexander the Great a ferocious hunting dog as a gift, but the dog was quite lazy and had no interest in hunting big game. Disgusted, Alexander had the dog killed. When the king heard that Alexander had killed this magnificent hunting dog, he sent another with a note suggesting that Alexander should not be "wasting the dogs' time with small things." Hearing this, Alexander pitted the dog against a lion. The dog swiftly broke the lion's back and destroyed it. Then he ran an elephant off a cliff, destroying it as well. So impressed was Alexander that from then on he used the breed in battle.

Skilos tou Alexandrou is reputed to be the strongest, most powerful Greek breed, completely fearless and devoted to its flock, fighting to the death. Through paintings and statues dating from approximately 3,000 BCE, these giant war dogs have been traced to Egypt, Persia, Mesopotamia, and Asia. It is said that Alexander the Great crossed the giant Macedonian and Epirian war dogs with the short-haired "Indian" dog to create the ferocious Molossus—the forefather of today's Neapolitan mastiff.[1]

> *An interesting side note: Historians suggest that as a result of the conquering wars of Alexander the Great and Genghis Khan, who destroyed everything in their path, including the largest library in the world (the Library of Baghdad), much of the history of the Afghan hound was destroyed.*

2. JULIUS CAESAR'S ARMY OF DOGS

Julius Caesar's mighty army included his armored dogs of war. Dressed in wide, iron-studded collars that protected their necks, the powerful dogs would charge toward the enemy, taking down man and horse and fighting to the death. So powerful, so ferocious, so large and ominous were these dogs that most foes turned and took flight at the mere sight of them.

Like Alexander the Great, Julius Caesar respected and understood the power of the war dog and presumably took part in selective crossbreeding. The Molossus—a Greco-Roman war dog—would eventually develop into the variety of mastiffs we know today. Not only did Julius Caesar use these dogs in times of

Author's Collection

The modern mastiff is a descendent of
war dogs from the ancient world.

war, he also enjoyed them for entertainment, pitting
them against bears, lions, tigers, stag, and boars in
arena fights. The ferocity with which they fought made
them real crowd pleasers.

But Caesar's pet of choice was the greyhound—
two greyhounds accompanied him as companions and
for hunting.[2]

3. THE BLACK PLAGUE AND THE BLACK DOG

After the fall of the Roman Empire, the status of the
dog took a negative turn. This was a brief, yet dark
period in canine history during which dogs held no
social status, no economic or family value, and were
left to fend for themselves. As large packs of dogs
scoured the countryside for food, the bubonic plague
began to spread in Europe. Two very unfortunate
things occurred—dogs had an inborn resistance to the

plague, and the starving and desperate dogs would eat whatever they could (which included the rotting bodies of the deceased who were not yet buried). Fleas carried by rats, dogs, cats, and other domesticated animals carried and spread the disease, cementing the notion that dogs (among other animals) were vile creatures.

Severe famine forced Europeans to take up arms in hopes of felling a stag, rabbit, boar, or anything else edible. As history has a way of repeating itself, the dog returned, proving to be a formidable foe of wild animals in the thick forests and marshes. A good hunting dog was again considered to be worth immeasurable wealth.

4. KING FOR THE DAY

During the eleventh century CE, a Norwegian king, furious at being deposed by his subjects, named his dog, Saur (or Suening), as new king. When the dog took the throne, the former king demanded that the animal be treated regally. For three days (although some accounts report it was three years), the dog served as King of Norway until it fought and lost to a bear.[3]

5. THE BEWITCHED BOY

The English Prince Rupert (1619–1682) was a handsome, victorious prince who was in the constant company of his dog, Boy. Because such good fortune had befallen the prince, and because he was always with the dog, people around the prince believed that Boy was, in fact, a witch in the form of a dog. As a commander in King Charles I's cavalry, Prince Rupert experienced his first major defeat on June 1, 1644, at

Marston Moor, when Boy was killed. While Prince Rupert was devastated, those around him were vindicated, believing their suspicions about the witch-dog had been correct. Although he was the victim, the prince was forever shrouded in controversy because he had kept company with a witch.[4]

6. HOW THE FRENCH REVOLUTION CHANGED THE DOG

Once upon a time, only kings, princes, knights, and other nobles of the time were allowed to hunt game. Dogs were a noted sign of prestige, so even the dog's breeding became extremely important. Rogue hounds were usually destroyed so that most commoners could never posses a dog of their own. Even those who did have a dog would not dare hunt for fear of being caught. As early as 1016, Canute the Great of Denmark and England issued a decree that any dog not belonging to nobility that was found on his royal hunting preserve should be caught and have its legs broken.

It was not until after the French Revolution that hunting became the right of ordinary citizens. The results of this were threefold. Dogs empowered people, raising their social status and allowing them to feed their families better. The policy also led to new, smaller hunting breeds. Because the average hunter was on foot, it became essential to have a hunting companion he could keep up with.[5]

7. BARRY AND NAPOLEON'S ARMY

In the mountains of the Great Saint Bernard, regal dogs served as guides and rescue dogs. Trained by monks, the breed moved easily through the snowy, mountainous region protecting travelers. Historian

Chrétien des Loges described how the dogs did "search the snow and find the way to those who are lost." As the French Revolution was drawing to a close and large numbers of troops traveled through the treacherous region, he reported, "At that time the dogs seem so well trained that from 1790 until 1810 not one single soldier died abandoned in the mountain. There was not a single victim amongst the forty thousand men of Napoleon's army who went through the Pass in May 1800."

Among these marvelous dogs was a special Saint Bernard named Barry, who, before he died, became one of the most famous dogs of his time. He saved more than forty people in his life, including a small boy buried by an avalanche. Barry licked the boy's face until he awoke, then somehow convinced him to climb on his back. Barry then carried the boy down the mountain to safety.

To this day, the most beautiful male Saint Bernard on the Great Saint Bernard is always called Barry.[6]

8. **BALTO**

In 1923, a Siberian husky named Balto was born in Nome, Alaska. Unlike the dog in the animated movie, *Balto*, this Balto was not half-wolf, half-dog but, like in the movie, he was considered unworthy of serving as a sled dog. However, when a diphtheria outbreak threatened the lives of many children, Balto was given his chance.

On January 21, 1925, a vaccine that was sent by train to prevent the epidemic made it only as far as Nenana, some 674 miles from Nome. Impossible weather conditions meant sled teams would have to attempt the journey to retrieve the medicine. Dozens of teams set out, but on February 1, 1925, Balto's team claimed the vaccine. Musher Gunnar Kassen made Balto lead dog and they began to navigate their way back to Nome—just as the blizzard took a turn for the worse. Miraculously, Balto found the trail and led his team and the vaccine to Nome—to a hero's welcome.

A statue of Balto stands in New York's Central Park with an inscription that reads: "Dedicated to the indomitable spirit of the sled dogs that relayed the toxin 600 miles over treacherous waters, through artic blizzards, from Nenana to the relief of stricken Nome in the winter of 1925—Endurance, Fidelity, Intelligence."

Today, the annual Iditerod Trail Sled Dog Race is run from Anchorage to Nome (since 1973), commemorating the sled dogs that have been a major part of life in Alaska, especially those who saved so many lives.[7]

9. LAIKO

Laiko, which means "barker" in Russian, was a Siberian husky mix stray found in Moscow. While there were many dogs in the Soviet space program, Laiko was slated to make history because of her ability to remain calm for long periods while being subjected to various tests.

On November 3, 1957, Laiko was hermetically sealed in the capsule, *Sputnik 2*, and launched into space, traveling at nearly eighteen thousand miles per hour for more than nine hundred miles above Earth's surface. Microphones were attached to Laiko's chest so that ground crews could monitor her heartbeats. Although she would go down in history as the first living being to orbit space, Laiko would never know of her achievements. Five to seven hours into the flight, there was no longer any sign of life; Laiko died of over-heating and stress. Her capsule/coffin circled the earth 2,570 times and burned up in the earth's atmosphere on April 4, 1958.

The data gathered from Laiko's journey provided information about what a living organism could tolerate and paved the way for humans to make that same trip.[8]

10.   LEWIS AND CLARK AND THEIR COMPANION, SEAMAN

On the historic Lewis and Clark expedition, a 150-pound Newfoundland named Seaman accompanied the party. This large, powerful dog was reputed to be an excellent swimmer, climber, watchdog, and companion on the journey. Seaman was noted to have "saved" various members of the expedition and was a respected member of the group. He was brave and stoic, but Seaman was also a Newfie through and through; he loved playing with his fellow explorers. His antics are included in the extensive diaries of the famous explorers.

Dogs of Royalty

Canine history details the evolution of the large breeds whose hunting skills fed entire families, fought wars, and destroyed enemies. But what of the smaller breeds? Just as the large breeds lived and traveled alongside pharaohs, kings, world leaders, and conquerors, so, too, did the little guys.

1. BEAGLE

The beagle is known to be one of the oldest breeds in the hound family used for the chase in the British Isles. It has been noted that Queen Elizabeth I kept "pocket" beagles, standing no more than ten inches at the shoulder, while King Charles II hunted with a pack on Newmarket Heath. Dwarf beagles were the preference of King George IV for hunting on Brighton Downs. The history of the beagle as a choice hunting companion endures today, as Prince Charles, among others, uses beagles for rabbiting in Windsor Great Park.

2. BICHON FRISE

This breed, weighing approximately seven to twelve pounds, was reintroduced to Europe from the Canary

Islands in the fourteenth century and became very popular in the fifteenth century at the royal courts. To own a bichon frise was a sign of great social standing among families of nobility or wealth.

3. CAVALIER KING CHARLES SPANIEL

The Cavalier King Charles received its name from Charles II, but this breed's reputation was established in European royal courts well before its sixteenth-century introduction into England. King Charles I was very fond of the spaniel and was rarely seen without his four-legged companions. It was a devotion that was shared by his children, Charles II, Henrietta, and James II. So devoted were these dogs, it was said that when Mary Queen of Scots was executed in 1587, her Cavalier King Charles spaniel had slipped beneath her skirts to be with her and was not discovered until after her death by her executioner.

In addition to serving as companions, these dogs are excellent hunters. The first Duke of Marlborough worked to develop a larger variety of the breed, known as the Blenheim, for hunting.

4. DACHSHUND

The dachshund first appeared in ancient Egypt and was depicted in Egyptian temples and tombs. Interestingly, early images of what is believed to be a dachshund have been found in carvings in Mexico. The dachshund reemerged on the royal scene in mid-1800s England. Prince Edward of Saxe-Weimar sent a small pack of smooth-haired dachshunds to Prince Albert, Victoria's Prince Consort, for pheasant hunting in Windsor Forest.

5. LHASA APSO

This breed is one of the world's most ancient dogs, dating back to 800 BCE. Developed from the Tibetan terrier and the Tibetan spaniel, the Lhasa apso was bred exclusively in Tibet, usually in monasteries. To ensure that reproduction of the breed remained under Tibetan control, very few dogs—only males—were given as gifts. Besides the lamas, only very high-ranking dignitaries were blessed with a Lhasa apso; said to symbolize the lion, they offered protection for Buddha and guarded monastic treasures.

6. MALTESE

Described by Greek philosopher Theophrastus as belonging to the "Melita" breed, the Maltese was a highly popular dog with royal families. The breed dated back to ancient Egypt, where it is believed Phoenician traders may have introduced it to Malta and the surrounding Mediterranean region. These small companions were a common sight on the thrones of kings and queens. A Maltese was a constant companion to none other than Queen Elizabeth I.

7. PAPILLON

The papillon is one of the oldest toy breeds in continental Europe, believed to have originated in Italy from the dwarf spaniel. It was a favorite of the French court, finding owners such as Marie Antoinette, Henry II, and Madame de Pompadour. Otherwise known as the "butterfly dog" due to the wide, erect positioning of its ears, the papillon was also very popular with artists of the time because it embodied wealth, class distinction, and social status. Rubens and Rembrandt portraits show papillons with their owners.

8. PEKINGESE

The history of this breed is legendary. Originating in Imperial China, the Pekingese can be traced back to the Han Dynasty, 206 BCE–220 CE. So protective of this breed were its original owners that only emperors, relatives, and courtiers at the Imperial Court were allowed to own one. Theft of a Pekingese was punished by execution. Upon the death of the master, the dog was sacrificed in the belief that he would continue to protect his owner in the afterlife. It was sometime after 1860 that the Pekingese was introduced to the rest of the world.

9. PUG

Royals Henry II of France, Marie Antoinette, Empress Josephine, and Britain's King William III, Queen Mary, and George III all enjoyed the pug's company. The pug was a favorite of the Victorian era. From historical references, we know that Queen Victoria had a favorite pug, "Bully"—a fawn—who was her constant companion.

Originally from the Orient, the breed was introduced to the West by traders from China. The late Duke and Duchess of Windsor were also avid pug lovers, and the breed continues to be a favorite with royals.

10. SHIH TZU

Like the Lhasa apso and Pekingese, the shih tzu was considered sacred in China; so sacred, in fact, that few details are known about its ancient roots. It is probably the crossbred result of the Tibetan temple dog, the Lhasa apso, and the early Pekingese. The Dalai Lama of Tibet offered the shih tzu in tribute to emperors. Until as late as the 1930s, these dogs were isolated behind the walls of the Forbidden City in Peking.[1]

Modern-Day Classifications

In 350 BCE, Aristotle made a list of known breeds, discussing their various physical traits and characteristics. Since that time, travelers, merchants, and warriors have crisscrossed the globe, taking their dogs with them and, thus, creating new and varied breeds.

By the nineteenth century, dog owners desired standards to classify the different breeds of dogs and their functions. In 1859, in the town hall of Newcastle upon Tyne in England, the first dog show took place. Although this first show was for hunting dogs only, it did demonstrate the importance of the role dogs had come to play in family, working, and cultural life. Ownership of popular breeds suggested a certain social standing.

In 1873, the English Kennel Club was formed, insisting on standards of genealogy and specific breed features such as height, weight, coloring, frame, and temperament. The American Kennel Club was created in 1884 and, five years later, the Italian Kennel Club.

While we are more accustomed to looking at the American Kennel Club (AKC) standards, it is fun to look at the Top Ten Classifications of the FCI, which recognizes more than four hundred breeds. The Federation Cynologique Internationale (FCI) coordinates, promotes, and protects cynology (canine behavior science) and purebred dogs among the international kennel clubs. (The AKC listing is included below.)

Category I: Shepherd, Guard, Defense, and Work Dogs

1. Shepherd
2. Guard dogs, defense

Category II: Hunting

3. Terrier
4. Dachshund
5. Hounds for Larger Game
6. Hounds for Smaller Game
7. Setters (with the exception of British Breeds)
8. English Hunting Dogs

Category III: Pet Dogs

9. All included

Category IV: Greyhounds

10. All included[1]

The American Kennel Club has broken down the category into seven groups: Sporting, Hound, Working, Terrier, Toy, Nonsporting, and Herding. Find your breed, along with the brief character description of the group it falls into.

Sporting

American Kennel Club's breed standards describe the temperament of the breed: "Naturally active and alert, sports dogs make likeable, well-rounded companions. Many of these breeds are remarkable for their instincts in the water and woods and actively continue to participate in hunting and other field activities. Potential owners of sports dogs need to realize that most require regular, invigorating exercise." The sporting breeds are: Brittany, pointer, German short-haired pointer, wirehaired pointer, Chesapeake Bay retriever, curly-coated retriever, flat-coated retriever, golden retriever, Labrador retriever, English setter, Gordon setter, Irish setter, American water spaniel, clumber spaniel, cocker spaniel, English cocker spaniel, English springer spaniel, field spaniel, Irish water spaniel, Sussex spaniel, Welsh springer spaniel, vizsla, Weimaraner, and wirehaired pointing griffon.

All of these dogs are trained to work in and around the water, in the fields, and with hunters. They are excellent companions who love to please their owners, but many of the bird dogs are notorious mouthers. They want and need to retrieve and carry the kill. They are very active—great for hunting, but hard on your couch. Find the proper outlet for your dog's energies and you will have a wonderful companion.

Hounds

As stated by the AKC breed standard, "Most hounds share the common ancestral trait of being used for hunting. Some use acute scenting [or sight] powers to follow a trail. Others demonstrate a phenomenal gift of stamina as they relentlessly run down quarry. Beyond this, however, generalizations are hard to come by

[because] the group encompasses quite a diverse lot."
They are: Afghan hound, basenji, basset hound, beagle, black-and-tan coonhound, bloodhound, borzoi,
dachshund, foxhound (American and English),
greyhound, harrier, Ibizan hound, Irish wolfhound,
Norwegian elkhound, otterhound, petit basset griffon
vendéen, pharaoh hound, Rhodesian ridgeback, saluki, Scottish deerhound, and whippet.

Hounds are extremely intelligent and hard-working
dogs, but they can be very difficult to train (basic obedience) simply because of their incredible instinct for
hunting/tracking. Although they are extremely affectionate and loyal to their owners, they can be difficult
to motivate for basic obedience. Needing more than
just praise, hounds work well in reward-based training
(treats) and require a lot of patience. Be consistent
and committed to training and you will have an excellent dog.

Working

The AKC breed standard says, "Dogs of the Working
Group were bred to perform such jobs as guarding
property, pulling sleds and performing water rescues.
They have been invaluable assets to man throughout
the ages: Quick to learn, these intelligent, capable animals make solid companions. Their considerable
dimensions and strength alone, however, make many
working dogs unsuitable as pets for the average families. Again, by virtue of their size alone, these dogs
must be properly trained." They are: Akita, Alaskan
malamute, Anatolian shepherd, Bernese mountain
dog, boxer, bullmastiff, Doberman pinscher, giant
schnauzer, Great Dane, Great Pyrenees, Greater
Swiss mountain dog, komondor, kuvasz, mastiff,
Newfoundland, Portuguese water dog, rottweiler, Saint

Bernard, Samoyed, Siberian husky, and standard schnauzer.

Like the Sporting Group, dogs in the Working Group can be immature and require a dedicated owner who is ready to work with them, giving consistent training and messages. Give a working puppy an inch and he'll take the whole yard. Once you have established yourself as top dog, however, and continue to give your dog positive, physical outlets for his energy, you will have a great friend.

Terrier

According to the AKC breed standard, "People familiar with this group invariably comment on the distinctive terrier personality. These are feisty, energetic dogs. Terriers typically have little tolerance for other animals, including other dogs. Their ancestors were bred to hunt and kill vermin. Many continue to project the attitude that they're always eager for a spirited argument. In general, they make engaging pets but require owners with the determination to match their dogs." They are: Airedale terrier, American Staffordshire terrier, Australian terrier, Bedlington terrier, border terrier, bull terrier, cairn terrier, Dandi Dinmont terrier, fox terrier (smooth and wirehaired), Irish terrier, Jack Russell terrier (aka Parson Russell terrier), Kerry blue terrier, Lakeland terrier, Manchester terrier (standard), miniature bull terrier, miniature schnauzer, Norfolk terrier, Norwich terrier, Scottish terrier, Sealyham terrier, soft-coated wheaten terrier, Staffordshire bull terrier, Welsh terrier, and West Highland white terrier.

The description given by the AKC breed standard sums this group up nicely. What is not mentioned is that *when* you are able to break through and lay down your own rules, *when* you are able to successfully train this dog, it is so rewarding. They are truly a pleasure to be and work with once the ground rules are set and understood. Good luck and enjoy. Be patient and consistent.

Toy

According to the AKC breed standard, "The diminutive size and winsome expressions of the Toy dogs illustrate the main function of this group: to embody sheer delight. Don't let their tiny stature fool you, though—many toys are tough as nails. If you haven't yet experienced the barking of an angry Chihuahua, for example, just wait. Toy dogs will always be popular with city dwellers and people without much living space." They are: affenpinscher, Brussels griffon, Cavalier King Charles spaniel, Chihuahua, Chinese crested, English toy spaniel, Havanese, Italian greyhound, Japanese chin, Maltese, Manchester terrier, miniature pinscher, papillon, Pekingese, Pomeranian, poodle, pug, shih tzu, silky terrier, and Yorkshire terrier.

So often owners do not think their little toys need training. It is easier to scoop them up and ignore the tiny barks. In truth, this is a stubborn and tough group that needs just as much training as the next group. These dogs are temperamental, with a wide range of characteristics—from very pleasant to difficult and stubborn—but they excel when given instruction and discipline.

Herding

As stated by the AKC breed standard, "All herding breeds share the innate ability to control the movement of other animals." They are: Australian cattle dog, Australian shepherd, bearded collie, Belgian Malinoise, Belgian sheepdog, Belgian Tervuren, border collie, Bouvier des Flanders, briard, Canaan dog, collie, German shepherd, Old English sheepdog, puli, Shetland sheepdog, and Welsh corgi (Pembroke and Cardigan).

You haven't seen anything until you have seen the intensity of a herding dog working his flock or herd. It is nothing short of amazing and proof of why it is so important to give these dogs structure, training, and regular exercise. Just watch a corgi work an unwilling herd of cows—how he nips and snaps to make the herd move. Dogs of this group crave difficult challenges, but even something as simple as throwing a ball a few minutes a day can greatly improve the mood and manners of an indoor herder. Training is a must.

Nonsporting

AKC breed standard reports, "Here are sturdy animals with [very] different personalities and appearances. Some such as the schipperke and Tibetan spaniel are uncommon sights in the average neighborhood. However, others, such as the poodle and Lhasa Apso have quite a large following. The breeds in the Non-Sporting Group are a varied collection in terms of size, coat, personality and overall appearance." They are: American Eskimo dog, bichon frise, Boston terrier, bulldog, Chinese shar pei, chow chow, dalmatian, Finnish spitz, French bulldog, keeshond, Lhasa apso, löwchen, poodle, schipperke, shiba inu, Tibetan spaniel, and Tibetan terrier.[2]

Dogs in Mythology

Dogs' roles in mythology are evident in Egyptian, Greek, and Scandinavian pottery, sculpture, and literature. In every way, they appeared to be part of the lives of modern humans. Gods and goddesses bore a resemblance to and/or the characteristics of dogs at the same time as dogs were depicted as lowly scavengers feeding on human flesh. In Homer's *Iliad* or in the epic poem, *Beowulf*, dogs are vicious man-eaters, guardians of the underworld, and, generally, thought to be dirty, vile, and evil. In the *Odyssey*, canines are recognized more as we know them today: as loyal, brave companions. Here, we meet ten of the most memorable canines in mythology.

1. ODYSSEUS'S ARGOS

When Odysseus left with the Spartan army to seize Troy, he left behind his faithful companion—the four-legged Argos. Twenty years came and went before Odysseus made his way back home. Exhausted and malnourished from his arduous journey, he was not recognizable. Disguised as a beggar, Odysseus sat at the entrance of his palace to reconnoiter his home. As he sat and pondered, he saw to his great surprise that his old friend, Argos, was still alive. Argos saw him, too. The old dog dragged himself to his feet, crossed the yard, and—covered with filth, matted fur, and flies—lay his head upon Odysseus's lap. His tail gave a final thump and he died. Argos had stayed faithful to his old friend Odysseus until his return.[1]

2. THE DOG DAYS OF SIRIUS

Sirius (Alpha Canis Majoris) represents Orion's larger hunting dog and is commonly referred to as the constellation, "Dog Star" or "Great Dog," because it is the brightest star in the sky. The Egyptians used Sirius to set their calendar because the movements of this constellation are connected to the change of seasons. According to the Egyptians, Sirius was not just important to life on earth but was critical as well to the "departed souls" of earth. We refer to the long, hot days of summer as "dog days" because Sirius marks their arrival.[2]

3. THE DOG AS A GOD

Thoth, the dog-headed ape, was the Egyptian god of writing, wisdom, learning, and the moon. It is said that Thoth invented the written word, authored the Book of the Dead, and was the vizier and scribe of the afterlife. It was Thoth who sat in judgment of the deceased and, upon his findings, he would summon the other dogs to help make the final decision about how the deceased should spend his or her afterlife. Thoth was depicted as a wise god, often holding scrolls, and a pen with which he documented all things.

With his wife, Ma'at, Thoth had eight children, including the god, Amon. A self-appointed god, Thoth was thought to have invented magic and the hermetic arts. Each day Thoth rose after sunset to drive away darkness.[3]

4. HERCULES'S TWELFTH LABORER

When Eurystheus ordered Hercules to go the underworld to kidnap the beast called Cerberus (aka Kerberos), it was certainly a suicide mission: Cerberus was a three-headed dog who guarded the entrance of Hades. It should be noted that in several accounts, Cerberus is said to have had fifty heads (fifty was a number of great magical power in mythology). Cerberus also had a serpent's tail and snake heads all over his body that devoured raw flesh.

The battle between Hercules and Cerberus was a fierce one, but Hercules eventually did overtake the beast and return to Eurystheus with his prize. Once his mission was accomplished, Hercules returned Cerberus to guard the gateway to the underworld.

5. DOG OF DEATH

In mythology, Anubis was the Egyptian god of death. Anubis was a black jackal or dog, two animals that have been associated with death throughout the history of humankind. He is also depicted as a man with the head of a dog or jackal. Whatever the image, this god was the overseer of souls, the color black representing the color of human corpses once they had undergone an embalming process.

The Anubis's parents were Re and either Nephthys or Isis. Anubis reigned until he was replaced by Osiris and took on the role as god of the funeral cult and the carer of the dead. In a similar role to that of Thoth, Anubis was often thought of as the "conductor of souls."[4]

6. THE GODDESS OF DOGS

The Greek goddess, Hecate, had a special affection for dogs (along with horses and lions) and was sometimes depicted as a dog-headed goddess. She also had a reputation—like the dog—that was less than desirable. This is likely because she associated with jackals and dogs. She was believed to wander graveyards and haunt dark nights with vicious hounds. It did not help that her pet dog was Cerberus.

But Hecate was also associated with the Dog Star, Sirius, and, like Thoth, was said to be a goddess of magic and the moon. No goddess better personifies the conflicting images of the dog than Hecate and her always-tumultuous relationships with the gods.

7. DOG OF DHARMA

In the Hindu epic, *Mahabharata*, Yudhishthira, king of Pandavas, sets out with his dog, five brothers, and their shared wife. The journey takes the group to the sacred *omphalos* (the center part or focal point) of the Hindus, Mount Meru, but is so perilous that all but one member dies of exhaustion. Only Yudhishthira and his dog survive. Yudhishthira "enters heaven through his mortal body, not having tasted death." His dog comes with him, and is revealed as Dharma (the Law) in disguise.[5]

8. THE GOLDEN DOG OF ZEUS

Kronos was the youngest of the Titanes and the God of Time as it affects the course of human life. The king of gods before Zeus, Kronos feared a prophecy that he would be overthrown by his son, so he swallowed each of his children when they were born. Rhea, his wife, saved the youngest, Zeus, feeding Kronos a stone instead. Fearing Kronos would discovery her deception, Rhea hid her son in the Kretan cave. Along with Zeus she sent a goat (Amaltheia) for milk, soldiers to protect the outside of the cave, and Kuon Khryseos, a golden dog to protect the goat.

Kuon Khryseos and Amaltheia remained loyal to Zeus throughout his life, and later, when Zeus drove out the Titanes and defeated Kronos, the goat was immortalized among the stars, and the Golden Dog was ordered to guard the sacred spot in Krete (Crete).[6]

9. HOUNDS OF HELL

Not nearly as noble as the story of Zeus are the mythological creatures in *Beowulf.*

The heroic epic describes the monster, Grendel and his mother as *werhdo*, *herorowearh*, *brimwulf*, and *grundwyrgenne*, all references to wolflike characteristics. Grendel is also denounced as *scucca,* synonymous with the phantom black dog, *Black Shuck*. Grendel and his mother are clearly depicted as canine or lupine demons who prowled the fenland and marshes, wreaking death and destruction. The human aspect of Grendel (something that has always been of great interest and an object of study among historians) connects them to the old Germanic idea of outlawry, or to the werewolf.[7]

10. AT THE HANDS OF MAN

No mythological tale better sums up how the dog has been undermined and misunderstood by humans, while remaining faithful and loyal, than "The Farmer and His Dog."[8]

Upon return to his home after repairing a fence, the farmer finds the cradle of his only child turned upside down. The cradle is destroyed and lying next to it is the bloodied and torn clothing of his child in his dog's mouth. Enraged, he crushes his dog's head with a hatchet. But when he overturns the cradle, he finds his child unharmed and lying next to him an enormous serpent—a beast that had been killed by the faithful dog that had saved his child.

Canines and Proverbs

1. Show a dog your finger, and he wants the whole hand.

   —Yiddish proverb

2. If you are a host to your guest, be a host to his dog also.

   —Russian proverb

3. A house without either a cat or a dog is the house of a scoundrel.

   —Portuguese proverb

4. To live long, eat like a cat, drink like a dog.
   —German proverb

5. The dog wags his tail, not for you, but for your bread.
   —Portuguese proverb

6. If you call one wolf, you invite the pack.
   —Bulgarian proverb

7. The greatest love is a mother's; then a dog's; then a sweetheart's.

   —Polish proverb

8. Live with wolves, and you learn to howl.
   —Spanish proverb

9. Beware of silent dogs and still water.
   —Latin proverb

10. The barking of a dog does not disturb the man on a camel.
    —Egyptian proverb[1]

Evolution of the Canine

1. **HOW CRUCIAL HAS THE ROLE OF HUMANS BEEN IN THE EVOLUTION OF WOLVES?**

Once a beautiful animal that roamed the earth, the wolf became one of a number of endangered species. The once symbiotic hunting partnership between wolves and humans changed radically with the rise of the domesticated dog. Suddenly, the wolf became the enemy as the domesticated dog moved into the camp, guarding humans and tending flocks. Today, wolves and humans are fearful of one another. Although twentieth-century literature would suggest otherwise, modern-day wolves are independent animals that prefer no contact with humans. There is no documentation of wolves hunting or killing humans, though the stories of frightening attacks have certainly made for good fiction. If left alone, wolves pose no threat to people. On the contrary, we humans have moved into their territory, depleting their food supply and threatening their very existence.

2. **HOW CRUCIAL HAS THE ROLE OF HUMANS BEEN IN THE EVOLUTION OF DOGS?**

Unlike the wolf, today's dogs are dependent on humans for survival, and they crave our attention and affection. Centuries of crossbreeding have diversified the dog's appearance and functions. From hunting partner and protector to pampered pet, we have bred a dog for every purpose. Traditional roles of hunting, herding, guarding, and rescue remain, but modern dogs do much more. They serve as helpers for the blind, deaf, disabled, and sick. They search for drugs, weapons, illegal plants, and even black mold.

Our canine friends have become integral to every part of our lives. However, in developing new breeds of dogs and expanding their functions, man has also created a problem in the dog world—overpopulation. In stark contrast to the dwindling numbers of wolves, there are now so many dogs in the United States that we euthanize thousands of them a day.

3. GIVEN A COMMON ANCESTRY, CAN'T THE WOLF AND DOG BREED? WHAT WOULD BE THE LIKELY RESULT OF A WOLF-DOG HYBRID?

Today, wolves, jackals, dogs, and coyotes can still interbreed and produce fertile offspring. While the jackal and coyote are generally considered pests and hold little appeal for today's humans, the notion of a wolf-dog cross has become increasingly popular. Many hybrid breeders are fighting to have this new cross recognized as a breed, but the reality is that wolf-dog hybrids are notoriously difficult to manage and can be very dangerous. Following the nature of their wolf ancestry, these crossbreeds are unpredictable. Most professional trainers, animal behaviorists, and veterinarians do not support this practice. Additionally, wolf researchers and enthusiasts object to bastardizing the wolf.

4. THE SOCIAL STRUCTURE OF HUMANS AND WOLVES/DOGS

Perhaps one of the reasons dogs and humans developed such an early yet strong relationship was that they understood each other. Both humans and wolves/early dogs lived in couples with a hierarchy. There was a leader (often male), and tribal/pack members who had specific jobs. One wolf would locate the track of a game animal; the pack would locate the animal; and one pack member would block or distract the prey while another would attack and bring the animal down. Similar social structures existed for wolves' eating, sleeping, mating, and playing. Early man could observe and respect the similarities between his social system and that of the wolves.

5. THE FIRST DOMESTICATED ANIMAL

The first animal to be domesticated by humans was the dog. Wolves, it is argued, made themselves known around the first campfires, begging for scraps. In doing so, they became territorial over such camps and their inhabitants, slowly taking over the role of guard dogs. They would bark when strange animals approached, warning the humans of impending danger.

The wolf showed itself to be a good hunting companion and was rewarded with leftover scraps and, probably, growing affection. As both humans and wolves evolved, so did their relationship. Early dogs became useful for herding, protection, hunting, and companionship. Unlike domestication of the horse or elephant, the dog never had to be forcibly captured and "broken in." Historically, this relationship has always been built on mutual understanding and respect.

An excavation site in Pompeii, the Roman city destroyed by Mt. Vesuvius in CE 79, revealed the remains of a dog lying over a small child, apparently trying to protect him. Even that early, the relationship between humans and our "best friend" was well in place.

6. THE FIRST KNOWN BREED

The "Peat Bog dogs" were the first named group of dogs—raised by the Neolithic palafitte dwellers in what is now Europe. During this period, new kinds of breeds emerged for hunting, shepherding, guarding, and other work. Whether these different kinds of dogs came from selective breeding by humans, or from genetic mutations due to climate or environment, the breeds became more distinct, allowing for later breed classifications.

However, the first fully recognized breed as we know it today is the saluki, a Persian greyhound, whose name means "noble." This breed is known to be friendly with children and family members, but it is also a strong hunter with incredible endurance. And, with its excellent sense of hearing, the saluki came to be known as a good watchdog. The concept of breeds and breed standards can be traced to the Persians, who took particular interest in breeding dogs and horses.

Today, the saluki is used to hunt gazelle in its native Persia (Iran) and continues to serve as a watchdog.[1]

7. AFTER CENTURIES OF HUMAN INTERVENTION, CAN TODAY'S DOG BE THE VIGILANT AND MIGHTY HUNTER IT ONCE WAS?

Most dog breeds and their purposes (herding, hunting, guarding, and companionship) were established well before the first century CE. Once upon a time we relied heavily on our dogs for safety, food, and comfort. Today, the need for herding and hunting has diminished, and using bird dogs or hounds on the chase is more for sport than anything else. Herding is now also a sport in many countries. This is not to say, however, that the canine's original senses have decreased. Dogs have the greatest sense of smell of all domestic animals, possessing about

280 million olfactory cells, compared to a human's twenty million cells. Tracking dogs can smell a six-week-old fingerprint on a pane of glass. A dog's hearing is equally impressive—picking up sounds from more than 250 yards away; most people cannot hear beyond twenty-five yards. We continue to use these impressive qualities beyond field and forest to help in search and rescue and to serve as helper dogs for people with diminished senses. If anything, dogs today are more vigilant and mightier than ever.

8. JUST HOW CLOSE ARE WE TO "MAN'S BEST FRIEND?"

While wolf-dog hybrid enthusiasts claim a close relationship between domesticated dogs and wolves of the wild, humans are actually closer to the social complexity of the domesticated dog. To get a more accurate understanding of this structure, behaviorists are studying the interactions of humans and dogs more than the interactions among wolves. Although the wolf pack is close, the human/dog relationship is proving to be very complex and very tight—much like human family life. How close are we really? Perhaps this is a clue: 3 percent of Americans admit to showering with their dogs at bath time.

9. WHY DOES MY DOG ROLL IN DIRT AS SOON AS HE'S HAD A BATH?

Biologists believe that rolling is an instinctive trait that may be rooted in the dog's sense of survival. By rolling in the dirt, the dog covers his scent and/or appearance to deceive predators or other competitors. For this same reason, it is not unusual for a dog to roll in manure or stinky garbage. Perhaps taking a shower with your dog will help.

10. **WHERE DID THE EXPRESSIONS, SUCH AS "IT'S A DOG'S WORLD," "DOG-TIRED," AND "HAIR OF THE DOG," COME FROM?**

After the fall of the Roman Empire—a time when dogs had been celebrated pets—when barbarians took over the land, dogs were tossed to the side and regressed to their packlike, prehistoric ancestry. It was during this time that large packs of hungry, roaming dogs scoured the countryside, causing a great deal of trouble and stirring fear in the hearts of many who would happen upon them. Historians believe that during this very negative period in canine history, many of today's expressions that reference dogs were born, including "son-of-a-bitch" and "die like a dog."

Canine Quotes

1. If you pick up a starving dog and make him prosperous, he will not bite you. This is the principal difference between a dog and a man.
   —Mark Twain

2. The more I see of the depressing stature of people, the more I admire my dogs.
   —Alphonse de Lamartine
   French poet (1790–1869)

3. They are better than human beings, because they know but do not tell.
   —Emily Dickinson

4. I've seen a look in dog's eyes, a quickly vanishing look of amazed contempt, and I am convinced that basically dogs think humans are nuts.
   —John Steinbeck

5. His name is not wild dog anymore, but the first friend, because he will be our friend for always and always and always.
   —Rudyard Kipling

6. A dog is like an eternal Peter Pan, a child who never grows old and who therefore is always available to love and be loved.

> —Aaron Katcher
> American educator and
> psychiatrist

7. A good dog never dies he always stays he walks beside you on a crisp autumn days when frost is on the fields and winter's drawing near, his head is within our hand in his old way.

> —Mary Carolyn Davis

8. Histories are more full of examples of the fidelity of dogs than of friends.

> —Alexander Pope
> English poet (1688–1744)

9. The poor dog, in life the firmest friend, "The first to welcome, foremost to defend."

> —Lord Byron
> Epitaph for his dog,
> Boatswain

10. Heaven goes by favor; if it went by merit, you would stay out and your dog would go in.

> —Mark Twain

II
Canines to the Rescue

Lucas and the Dogs of September 11th

Meet Mike Palumbo. He'll tell you all about his nine-year-old black Labrador retriever named Lucas and the work they did together in New York City on the days that followed September 11, 2001. He'll also tell you again and again how Lucas is no different from the other search and rescue dogs of September 11th or any other recovery mission at a disaster site. Because of his tremendous respect for dogs—his and those of all his comrades—he refuses to let Lucas take any undo credit. Lucas, Palumbo would tell you, is just one of hundreds of dogs who worked the devastation in New York and Washington, D.C. And so, let this be the story of just one dog from so many who tried so hard to bring closure to a terrible day in history. Meet Lucas.

On the morning of September 11, 2001, like most Americans, Mike Palumbo was watching the unimaginable. From his office at the Union County (Ohio) Sheriff's Department, he watched the first of the Twin Towers fall. In the next hour, he received a page from the Federal Emergency Management Agency (FEMA) (all FEMA rescue specialists must carry a pager at all times). As a member of Ohio Task Force One, Palumbo was given his six-hour window to take care of personal affairs, pack his gear, and deploy. He made three phone calls: to his oldest daughter, his wife, and his vet.

"[The vet] literally met me in the lobby of her office to give Lucas a quick check. When I got home, I started to get my uniform on, and Lucas knew we were getting ready to work. They are such masters of body language. He just knew."

By 7 p.m. on September 12, 2001, Palumbo and Lucas were standing at Ground Zero, looking at something neither had ever encountered before. "It was hard to comprehend," says Palumbo. "The vastness, the enormity," as he searches for the right words, there is a notable strain in his voice. "I've been to some disaster sites, but this . . . I thought, 'Where do we start?'"

They did, working twelve-hour shifts with much-needed breaks every twenty to thirty minutes to get water, cool off, and try desperately to detach themselves from what was actually happening. Even when the teams returned to the Jacob Javits Convention Center, "our home while we were there," they tried not to hear the personal stories about those who had lost their lives or were still missing. The teams tried to remain professional, objective, and focused, but that would be impossible.

And it was clear that the dogs were being used for so much more than search and rescue efforts. "Whatever you needed for a dog, the people of New York would move heaven and earth to get it." The dogs gave people hope and encouragement, but something else as well, Palumbo explains.

"There were times when we would talk to the firefighters," he says, "we'd be resting between searches, and ask, 'Did you lose anyone?'" Always, the firefighters reached out to the dogs for comfort, often petting them, averting eye contact with others, and feeling the soothing warmth that only a dog in the greatest disaster in American history could offer. Palumbo recalls that one of the firemen was searching for a member of his company—a man with whom he had switched shifts. "The dogs were just a great relief to so many. They [the firefighters] would come over to pet our dogs, and you could see it in their eyes. They would come over and hug the dogs. They just needed to sit down, take a break, and pet the dogs. One guy who was petting Lucas said, 'Boy, I miss my dog. I mean, I miss my wife, too, but I really miss my dog.'" Man's best friend—in time of need.

The days were long and hard. It was necessary for the handlers to set up live rescues for all the dogs. At the end of each day, Palumbo would see to it that Lucas found a victim—one who would just happen to have his very favorite toy, a rolled towel, and who would play tug-of-war with him after being saved. "We learned a lot after the Oklahoma City bombing," Palumbo says, noting that dogs become depressed when finding only lifeless bodies. Although Lucas never found a body one way or the other, the smell of death—a smell the dogs understand—was everywhere.

When the two would stop for a break, Palumbo would take off his gear, including his helmet, put Lucas in a down-stay and go off to get water. "Lucas would lay his head in my helmet for my scent, thinking, 'Daddy's coming back.'"

Thankfully, Lucas never sustained any life-threatening injuries. But what makes his story—like those of all the other dogs—so extraordinary is that he was there for us. Here are ten things you may have never known about these amazing and wondrous animals.

Author's Collection

Lucas, Mike Palumbo's search-and-rescue dog
that helped locate victims at the destroyed
World Trade Center after September 11, 2001.

1. THE DOGS

A wide variety of dogs—purebred and mixed—are used for search and rescue. Contrary to popular belief, dogs are not prejudged by their breed but, rather, by their individual personalities. According to FEMA, thousands of people called after September 11th, offering to send their dogs to New York and Washington, D.C. While the sentiment was appreciated, only very select dogs made the cut.

2. THE BREEDS

Among the breeds deployed in response to the attacks of 9/11 were: German shepherds, Australian shepherds, Belgian shepherds, Labrador retrievers (yellow, black, and chocolate), golden retrievers, Portuguese water dogs, German short-haired pointers, Belgian Malinois, border collies, Belgian Tervuren, Doberman pinschers, giant schnauzers, rat terriers, and several mixed breed dogs and "pound puppies."

> *An aristocrat among us:* Fearghas, a descendant of Rin Tin Tin, and his handler, Beth Barkley, were among the search and rescue teams at the Pentagon following September 11, 2001. Fearghas is a white German shepherd.

3. THE AMERICAN RESCUE DOG ASSOCIATION (ARDA)

In 1961, a little girl was lost with two family dogs in Snohomish, Washington. One dog remained with the lost child while the other went home and, with the encouragement of the family, was able to lead them back to the little girl. Her parents, Bill and Jean Syrotuck, were fascinated with the dog's abilities. As members of the German Shepherd Dog Club of Washington, they set out to train dogs to locate lost people, and the Search Dog Committee was formed. This was the beginning of the ARDA as we know it today.[1]

4. FEMA AND THE OKLAHOMA CITY BOMBING

The term, "Golden 24," refers to the time frame (the first twenty-four hours) during which most disaster survivors are found. FEMA's search and rescue dogs were given their first big test with the bombing of a federal building in downtown Oklahoma City in 1995. Created in the early 1990s, FEMA's urban search and rescue task force responded and went to work.

5. PHYSICAL REQUIREMENTS OF THE SEARCH AND RESCUE DOG

Double-coated dogs or, dogs with a thick undercoat, are ideal because their coat can serve as a natural insulation against the weather—hot or cold. These dogs must be agile enough to be transported easily in helicopters or to work in tight areas, but large enough to handle rough terrain. Few search dogs wear "booties" when working a rubble pile because they aren't able to maneuver as well, plus there is the concern that booties (and collars) will catch on broken debris. The dogs are taught a "soft walk" in which they are able to traverse broken glass and sharp metal.

6. THE EMOTIONAL STATE OF THE SEARCH AND RESCUE DOG

These dogs are hungry for the search. Search and rescue dogs are incredibly intelligent, driven dogs with the innate ability (or passion) to search and search and search, without becoming disheartened, distracted, or bored. These are extremely playful puppies who love to please and have a strong bond with their handlers. Approximately 85 percent of FEMA search and rescue canine handlers are civilian volunteers who consider their dogs to be "family dogs."

7. QUALIFYING AS A TEAM

The notion of becoming a search and rescue team may seem glamorous, but the hours, work, and dedication involved are rigid and demanding. Handler certification involves written and verbal tests regarding search and rescue strategies, briefing and debriefing skills, and canine handling. Dogs must be able to respond to commands, be agile and able to bark to signal a find, have a willingness to overcome fear under the guidance of the handler, and the skill to move efficiently and effortlessly in unfamiliar surroundings.

8. BEYOND THE RESCUE EFFORT

Rescue dogs have helped law enforcement officials solve crimes, including determining whether a crime has been committed. In one instance, builders unearthed a skull and were concerned that they had found a victim of foul play. Using search dogs, they discovered more and more bones. Anthropologists searched the areas where the dogs alerted and determined that they were standing on the site of a cemetery.

9. LIVE-FIND DOGS AND CADAVER DOGS

The live-find dog must be able to ignore people walking around the disaster site and use their air-scent training to concentrate on searching for living victims trapped beneath collapsed buildings and debris. This also means that the dogs must ignore the deceased.

But the work of the cadaver search dog is equally important. Air-scent trained dogs can locate the remains of a human weeks and even months after death. When the initial search begins, most teams hope to find the victim alive. While this is the outcome everyone wants—dogs included—finding the body of the deceased eases the victim's family's pain of not knowing what has happened to the loved one. Like live-find dogs, cadaver dogs are rewarded with praise, love, and playtime after a body has been found so they remain reliable, competent search dogs.[2]

10. THE RISKS INVOLVED FOR SEARCH AND RESCUE DOGS

Whether it is in the wilderness or at declared disaster sites, these courageous dogs put their bodies at risk to do what they love. Burns, drowning, fractures, dislocations, heatstroke, hypothermia, frostbite, puncture and bite wounds, hemorrhaging, and shock are all risks these teams take each time they set out to search and rescue. With each rescue, teams become better prepared, learning how to handle rescue/searches. Despite the hazardous conditions in New York following 9/11, few canine injuries were reported. As with the Oklahoma City bombing, stress was the number one ailment. This is significant, because the 9/11 disaster saw the largest deployment of search dogs in U.S. history, with more than four hundred dogs around the nation serving in time of need.

Search and Rescue Dogs in Times of Disaster

After September 11th, the perception of dogs was changed forever for thousands of people who really didn't like them all that much. In a time of total despair, search and rescue dogs offered hope and, as many would later report, crowds would part like the Red Sea at the words, "Dog coming through!" The dogs, everyone knew, were our greatest hope of finding survivors. But they do so much more than that.

In the past, search and rescue dogs have been used to find missing persons, avalanche victims, and criminals on the Pits Donrun. The bombing in Oklahoma City began to make believers out of the biggest dog cynics. As you will read, the Oklahoma City bombing dogs worked to exhaustion in hopes of finding survivors. Then, in the days following September 11th, we saw again how many dogs put their lives on the line for people they never knew. The spirit of the search and rescue dog is unmatched by that of any other canine. The following are just a few examples of how dogs have served us in time of need. FEMA handler Sonja Heritage shares some of her experiences as she and her German shepherd, Otto, worked some of the most devastating disasters of our time.

1. THE ARMENIAN EARTHQUAKE

In 1988, Russia's territory of Armenia was devastated by an earthquake that registered 6.9 on the Richter scale. Forty-five thousand people were killed, and millions more were left homeless. It is believed to be one of the worst disaster sites in history. Immediately, health care workers had two concerns—locating the living and reuniting them with family and the health needs in finding and properly caring for the deceased. Both the United States and France sent search and rescue teams. The French teams were assembled and sent almost immediately. Their dogs alerted their handlers to more than sixty people buried under the rubble. After some time, the dogs were used only as cadaver dogs. For many people, this was the first time dogs were seen in such a useful role, and the Armenians,, who were desperately hoping the dogs could find their lost parents, siblings, and children, treated them with great kindness.

2. OKLAHOMA CITY BOMBING

On April 14, 1995, an explosion ripped apart the Alfred P. Murrah building in Oklahoma City, Oklahoma. As people began their early morning routines, Timothy McVeigh parked a truck, filled with explosives powerful enough to wipe out one side of the structure, next to the building. More than one hundred people were killed. FEMA and ARDA instantly put teams to work. Although search and rescue dogs had long been used to find missing persons or to work disaster sites around the world, this was America's first real look at search and rescue dogs at home. The media began to focus on the dogs, and the public waited breathlessly as the animals were sent in and out of the building, hoping to find survivors. It would also be the public's first look at the dogs as they are—compassionate and loving. We saw them becoming depressed as they found only the deceased. National magazines ran pictures of dogs needing and giving hugs and, in the midst of such horror, an American icon was born.

3. THE EMBASSY BOMBING IN NAIROBI

When Sonja Heritage got the phone call that the American embassy in Nairobi had been bombed, it was the first mission she and Otto, her German shepherd, would work together. On August 7, 1998, terrorists attacked the U.S. embassy, killing dozens of U.S. and Nairobi citizens. Although Heritage and Otto had trained extensively for this moment, there was no way they could have been prepared for what lay ahead. One of the most daunting surprises was the smell. As Heritage reports, the combination of burned concrete, gasoline, oil, explosives, and sheer panic in the air remains most vivid in her mind. There were no live finds on their first mission.

"But he [Otto] did make some recovery finds. At first, we were both overwhelmed. There is so much more needed on a mission than you train for. The debris was waist high." Briefly, Heritage lost Otto in an elevator shaft. Working on blind faith and pure skill, Otto did what he was trained to do. Because most of the people in Nairobi had only been exposed to (unfriendly) police dogs, few residents made an attempt to pet Otto or any of the other canine rescuers.

4. EARTHQUAKE IN TURKEY

At 3 a.m. on August 17, 1999, Turkey was hit with an earthquake that registered 7.4 on the Richter scale.

Building floors fell down, one on top of the other, while people slept. Again, the U.S. mobilized search dogs, and teams were there in less than twenty hours. Working in one hundred-degree heat, dogs were often sent to the top of rubble, picking their way through the piles in search of survivors. The combined teams found more than a dozen people alive—people who would otherwise have died from dehydration and their injuries. In a place where dogs had frequently been thought of as scavengers, the people of Izmit, Turkey, were suddenly indebted to the canine teams.

For Heritage, the experience was extremely emotional. "When the people would see a dog, they would beg us to look where they had been before the collapse. There was a mother looking for her baby, but we just couldn't find anyone. It was heartbreaking and frustrating." Then, eighteen feet deep, Otto had his first live find. He began yapping and whining. Instantly, another dog was called for and run over the same area. The second dog confirmed Otto's find, reacting the same way. Listening devices were then used. "We didn't want to cause a secondary collapse," Heritage explains. Before any digging could begin, rescuers wanted to listen for signs of life. Sure enough, an air pocket within a stairwell revealed a human. Alive. "It was wonderful!" says a proud Heritage.

5. 1999 TAIWAN EARTHQUAKE

On September 20, 1999, more than two thousand people were believed to be dead when an earthquake registering 7.6 hit Taiwan. Thousands were reportedly missing and thought to be trapped beneath layers of rubble. The working dogs faced a new challenge because most of the apartment buildings were completely covered in ceramic tiles, making the surface incredibly slippery and dangerous. Makeshift ladders and climbing ropes were designed to get the dog teams on top of the piles so they could begin their search. All the highly motivated dogs wanted was to get on top of the piles to sniff out possible life. "The dogs were crying and whining to get on top. They didn't care that we were hauling them up by rope," Heritage says. After searching for one full week, the teams returned to their hotel in Taipei, preparing to return to the United States, when a powerful aftershock rocked the city, causing a hotel evacuation and the news that they had been reactivated to the city of Miencheng, where a twelve-story building had collapsed onto a highway.

6. AMERICA'S WORST DISASTER

At 8:46 a.m. on September 11, 2001, an airplane was flown into the North Tower of the New York City's World Trade Center (WTC), causing huge destruction. Minutes later, a second plane struck the South Tower, and the world as we had once known it was changed forever. Immediately rescue teams were set into motion—search and rescue dogs were an important part of these efforts. FEMA, ARDA, and K-9 units worked along twisted and burning metal, jagged pieces of glass, and stifling soot and ash in search of survivors. Many times dogs were sent into small crevices, disappearing from sight (and sound) for long periods. Remarkably, they always found their way back in the dark—unfortunately, however, with no sign of survivors. Reportedly, there was added pressure on the dog-handler teams because, not only family members, but police and firefighters as well would ask search teams to comb specific areas for a lost family member.

Even when they did not find survivors, the dogs were very good at indicating human remains. But what most police officers, firefighters, volunteers, handlers, and bystanders remember most about the dogs is how they also played the role of therapist. Indeed, media images portrayed private conversations between exhausted firefighters and the dogs.

7. CADAVER WORK FROM THE WORLD TRADE CENTER

Working a landfill site at Staten Island, dogs and handlers were outfitted in hazardous material suits, complete with boots, respirators, and helmets, to work specific sections. Supplied with buckets, the teams were asked to find human remains. As debris came in by the truckloads, the dogs and their handlers worked day and night. These trained dogs searched for tiny bits of bone, bodily fluid, and/or tissue among the rubble.

8. THE PENTAGON—SEPTEMBER 11, 2001

As staff members inside the Pentagon sat speechless at the sight of the World Trade Center under attack on CNN, they felt the hit. Most report they knew at once that they were under attack, while others actually saw the explosion from inside the building. Remarkably, one of the main points of impact had been under reconstruction, and those offices were still vacant. But for almost twenty-four hours, a number of people were unaccounted for. Search and rescue dogs were called in immediately. Just as at the WTC, the search would not include rescue. And just like New York, the dogs would play more than just the role of rescue worker; they would provide comfort to so many other rescuers.

In the aftermath of the attack, a woman named Susan Brewer put together a celebrity-packed event, called American Heroes of Freedom, as a way to commemorate the heroes of September 11th and begin the process of healing. Otto was front and center. "We were never alone," says Heritage. "Everybody came up to hug the big fuzzy dog. They could tell him [Otto] anything. Dogs are so healing."

9. CADAVER SEARCH IN THE PARKING LOT

Using the north parking lot as the search area for Pentagon debris, rakers moved through slowly in hopes of finding human remains. Dogs made the final sweep, finding anything from hair and tissue to bone and teeth. And just as at the New York site, dogs who had been trained to bark only with a live find, began to use different signals to alert their handlers to a cadaver find—a jerk, a sidestep, sitting down.[1]

(For more information about the incredible work of search and rescue dogs, go to www.fema.org or read *Search and Rescue Dogs: Training the K-9 Hero* by the American Rescue Dog Association, Howell Books, 2002.)

10. THE SPACE SHUTTLE DISASTER

The space shuttle, *Columbia*, broke up on reentry into the atmosphere over Texas on February 1, 2003, killing all seven crew members. As devastating as this was, it was also incredibly difficult to search for and gather remains and shuttle pieces. East Texas proved to be very challenging for Federal Bureau of Investigation (FBI) and National Aeronautics and Space Administration (NASA) officials because it is heavily overgrown with mesquite trees and brush. Few people are aware of the role dogs played in recovering pieces of the shuttle and human remains. Search and rescue dogs were used to search for remains, and many farm dogs reportedly discovered and carried home bits of the shuttle.

How You Can Prepare Your Dog for a Disaster

Who could have foreseen September 11th, much less planned for it? Still, thousands of animals needed rescuing after that disastrous day. But even for families that know a disaster is coming, such as a tornado or hurricane, there isn't always enough time to prepare family members—two-legged or four-legged—for a fast, safe exit. Rescue agencies and veterinarians recommend being prepared for the worst of situations for the sake of your pet.

1. HAVE A PLAN

Devise a plan so that you and your family will know what to do in the event of a fire, illness, or natural disaster. If you live in a floodplain or earthquake zone, know what to do, where to go, and where and how you will transport your animal(s). If you have a written list of instructions, should you be injured or taken ill, caregivers will know what to do with your dog.

2. TALK TO YOUR VETERINARIAN

It is equally important to know the plans your vet has made. In the event of an emergency, what are the vet's plans in terms of servicing the community? What will office hours be? Should something happen to the vet's established office, where should you seek care?

3. USE PROPER IDENTIFICATION

Every year, after powerful storms sweep through small towns and cities, hundreds of scared animals are on the run, confused, and, sometimes, hurt. For this reason, it is important that your dog carry current identification so that either you or your veterinarian can be located.

4. MEDICAL RECORDS

By keeping your pet's medical records current, there will be no question about the animal's health and medical status. This record should also include all possible emergency contact numbers for you—even if this means giving the telephone number of your mother, who lives on the other side of the country. Keeping your pet current on all shots will prevent any confusion over or inconvenience for your dog.

5. RESTRAINING YOUR DOG

All too often, dog owners are ill-prepared to properly restrain frightened or injured animals in the event of an emergency. Owning a portable crate, extra lead, and harness/collar is wise, as is as keeping an extra lead in the car with the emergency kit.

6. FOOD STORAGE

Keep at least a four-day supply of food and water on hand for your pets. Using several ziplock bags for food, you can recycle it every two to three months to keep it fresh. If your dog takes a prescription medication, be sure to have an extra supply in case of emergency.

7. FIRST AID KIT

Along with the food supply, be sure to have a first aid kit that includes bandages and medications for animals as well as a guide for administering pet care. Ask your vet for a list of supplies needed to fill your first aid kit.

8. AN ALTERNATE PLAN FOR CARE

In a moment of crisis, you do not want to be hunting for names, addresses, and phone numbers of other medical facilities and veterinarians. Make a list and call to speak to other veterinarians about receiving care in the event you are unable to contact your own veterinarian. Also compile a list of other caregivers, such as dog walkers and pet sitters, should you or anyone else in your family be unable to care for your dog.

9. CONSIDER PET HEALTH INSURANCE

Once the disaster is over, the cost is often far more than anyone can afford. Some medical insurance plans offered to pet owners may relieve additional financial burden during a time of crisis.

10. GIVE AND TAKE

Be prepared to help neighbors, friends, and coworkers when they are sick, traveling, or in need of assistance. Exchange pet information, including names, medical needs, feeding times, favorite toys, and walking schedules. Research shows that people in hospitals heal far more quickly when they know their pets have proper care.

Dogs in Prison

In prisons across the United States, and in many foreign countries, inmates are providing love and care to puppies and learning trust, responsibility, and self-respect. As part of a program to raise and train service dogs, prisoners are proving to be a dependable group of trainers who are able to spend considerable time with their dogs and are eager to participate in a growing service project.

Started in 1981 by Dominican nun Sister Pauline Quinn, the prisoners with pets programs in virtually every state provide service dogs that do everything from switching on lights to fetching medicine and opening doors to calling for help on special 911 telephones to acting as seizure alert dogs. Sister Pauline's childhood abuse and homelessness was the catalyst for her prisoner-pet partnership idea. Having been helped to recover emotionally by a dog, she believed that institutionalized women and men could gain hope and confidence from a relationship with "man's best friend." In today's programs, participants serve as first owners, raising puppies that eventually enter special training programs for blind, hearing-impaired, disabled, or sick owners. Some programs' members do part of the actual training.

Here are ten programs that serve as examples of the hundreds of prisoners who are learning to share, to serve, and to respect themselves and others.

1. **MISSOURI'S "DOG HOUSE"**

Twelve women in the maximum security prison near Vandalia, Missouri, eagerly await the weekly visits from their group of seven service dogs-in-training. The inmates, most of whom are in prison for murder, have three dogs living with them during the year-long training. In addition, each week, the other seven come to the prison for special training sessions. Laughter, baby talk, and lots of hugging greet the dogs. Although the training sessions are serious work, it is obvious that everyone—trainers and trainees—is having a good time. The women said that working with the dogs makes them feel like real people again. One prisoner summed up the feelings of the group about the importance of working with service dogs: "To give something back of such magnitude, you know your heart is going out those gates to somebody else."[1]

2. **INDIANA'S SERVICE DOGS TEACH TRUST**

Indianapolis television station WRTV aired a news story on April 15, 2002, about incarcerated adolescents and adults who are learning to train dogs to help people in need. The program started at the Pendleton Boys' School, where teenagers took to the training project, bonded with the dogs, and began to demonstrate commitment to and trust in others. The program has spread, and the service dogs are now in residence at the Girls' School, the Rockville Women's Prison, and the Indiana Women's Prison.

3. KANSAS'S GREYHOUNDS BEHIND BARS

A special training program is taking place in the Ellsworth (Kansas) Correctional Facility: Prisoners adopt and train retired greyhounds to be family members. Working with greyhound rescue groups, the prisoners give the dogs the love and socialization they may never have had while they were racing. The male inmates who work with the dogs learned quickly that racing dogs do not know how to act as pets. They have lived in kennels all of their lives. They often do not know how to climb stairs and do not recognize a window as a barrier, frequently walking into one. So, the dogs live with their trainers in the men's cells and often stay with the men throughout the day, even when the men are working, for the eight-week training session. The trainers report that they love working with the dogs and seeing them become "regular pets." In addition, the other prisoners, who were initially skeptical about having the dogs around, all stop to pet and talk to the canine residents.

4. OKLAHOMA'S FRIENDS FOR FOLKS

At the medium security unit of Lexington Correctional Center, some of the inmates have four legs. Rescued stray, abandoned, and abused dogs come to live with prisoners—one dog with a group of four prisoners. The dogs spend ten weeks or so with their groups, learning social and obedience skills; then, they become companions for the elderly and/or disabled. The inmates report that it is tough to see their dogs go, but the reward is knowing how happy the new owners will be. One of the prison guards talked about an Australian shepherd that the inmates trained for a little boy with cerebral palsy. When the boy and his mother came to meet the dog and his trainers, the dog got up and walked straight up to the boy, and you couldn't separate them from that moment on. The guard commented, "That will put a knot in your throat. It's what the program is all about."

5. ALASKA'S SLED DOGS: SOME SIT OUT THE IDITAROD IN PRISON

Sled dogs that cannot finish the grueling eleven hundred-mile Iditarod sled race may find themselves in jail. No, they are not being punished; they are being rescued. Since 1980, inmates at men's and women's correctional facilities along the Eagle River have taken in dogs that become sick, injured, overheated, or just cannot make the rest of the race. By the end of the race, the prisons may have two hundred dogs being cared for and loved by the inmates. Prison personnel report that inmates work to earn the privilege of being handlers and look forward all year to having the dogs come. As much care as the dogs receive, they give back in affection and companionship, once again helping their human companions beyond measure.

6. OHIO'S "DEATH ROW DOGS"

Inmates at the Richland and Mansfield (Ohio) Correctional Institutes raise and train dogs that were destined to be euthanized. The program, which brings dogs from various rescue groups to the prisons, is called Res-Q-1 Adoption. Puppies and adult dogs live with inmate trainers for seven weeks, during which time the dogs are schooled, socialized, and loved. The dogs are housebroken, leash-trained, socialized toward other dogs and strangers, and receive basic and advanced obedience training. When they are ready, Res-Q-1 Adoption matches the pups with new families (from a long waiting list), taking into account each family's wants and needs and each dog's nature and needs. The prisoners hate to see their charges leave, but they know each one will be placed in a good home, and a new pup in need of love and guidance will be living with them again soon.

7. MAINE'S DOWN EAST SERVICE DOGS

Some inmates in Maine correctional facilities considered themselves lucky men. They are doing something (they say) that has brought meaning and purpose into their lives, something that makes them look forward to the next day, the next year—they are training dogs. The Prison Dog Project trains prisoners to raise and train service dogs for the disabled and/or the blind. When assistance and guide dogs are raised from puppyhood and trained by the inmates, the time that a disabled or blind person has to wait for a dog is greatly reduced. Dogs of all ages live with their inmate trainers, with older, near-graduation dogs often helping to train the puppies.

8. WASHINGTON'S PRISON PET PARTNERSHIPS

At the Washington State Correctional Facility for Women, inmates train service, therapy, and seizure alert dogs. Not only do people in need benefit from the partnerships that provide assistance dogs, the program also helps the inmates learn how to be "other" centered, responsible, and patient. In addition, the women often say that they hope to use the training skills they learn to help them get jobs when they leave prison. There is yet another advantage: Prisoners who have participated in the thirteen-year partnership program have a recidivism rate of zero.

q. MASSACHUSETTS PRISON DOG PROGRAMS BUILD BRIDGES

Service dog training programs are popular in the Massachusetts prison system, as is the case in many other states and countries. In Massachusetts, prisoners, guards, prison administrators, and community members mention three particular results of the programs: the dogs bring a sense of calm to the institutional setting; they build a bridge between the inmates and the guards; and the programs build bridges between the institution and the surrounding community.

10. WISCONSIN'S LIBERTY DOGS

In 1997, the Sanger B. Powers Prison established the first service dog training program in a correctional facility in the state. An old farm shop on the grounds of the minimum security site was remodeled to serve as the training center and kennel. With a great deal of support from the local community, the program was up and running within a few months. The prisoner-trainers and their dogs provide physically challenged people in Wisconsin and upper Michigan with assistance and companionship and are, in the words of program personnel, "growing as a group and giving something of great value back to our community."

HONORABLE MENTION:

At the Stonewall Jackson Youth Development Center in Concord, North Carolina, youth offenders also work with puppies (rescued from animal shelters) in need of training. In exchange, the boys, ranging in age from twelve to seventeen, learn a new vocation. More important, says pet therapist coordinator Missy Overton, "The boys learn empathy and greater communication skills." The success rate of those chosen boys successfully integrating back into society is 90 percent.

Overton welcomes visitors and can be reached at 704-786-9163.

Sometimes the dogs are the prisoners. A high-security jail in Berlin is Europe's first rehabilitation jail for dangerous dogs. Stray fighting dogs and pets deemed by the courts to be a danger to the public are sent to the Berlin Interment Home. Each dog has an individual rehabilitation program that includes obedience training, obstacle courses, and chasing sticks. The jail's trainer says that most dogs can be "put on the straight and narrow." Those that cannot are euthanized. The jail is in a secret location because of owners who threaten jail personnel and, according to an official, "try to break into the prison to free their animals."

K-9s in Law Enforcement

Not only do our dogs give us love and companionship, provide us with laughs, and keep us healthier than we would probably be without them, they also protect us. Beyond acting as our own private security system—warning us when strangers or errant squirrels come too near our homes—dogs serve to keep our communities safe. Hundreds of Labradors, German shepherds, Doberman pinchers, golden retrievers, Belgian Malinois, bloodhounds, and even beagles work in police departments throughout the country— indeed, throughout the world. With their human police partners, the K-9 cops track and capture criminals, protect citizens and police, locate missing children and people in trouble, identify the whereabouts of evidence (including narcotics and explosives), perform crowd control, and save lives (often losing their own).

Every law enforcement officer can tell stories of brave and dedicated police dogs. The stories could fill a small library. Here are a few of them, told in honor of both the dogs that are the stars of the stories and all those that serve (and have served) with equal courage and honor.

1. FRANKO

Franko, a German shepherd, and his partner, Deputy Tedd Betts, have been honored by the American Red Cross for their bravery and quick action in a wide search for a woman who had threatened to commit suicide. Alerted by family members, the police and volunteers in Lewis, Washington, were conducting a hurried hunt for the woman, looking in every logical location. Franko branched out, tracking the missing woman's scent, and found her lying in a field, bleeding. He alerted his partner, who instantly called emergency medical units. Medical personnel attributed their ability to save the woman's life to the quick actions of Franko and Deputy Betts.

2. KYLIE

Trained as a scent dog, Kylie (a yellow Labrador) works with partner Deputy Gary Hall in Lake County, California. Kylie can identify numerous drugs, including marijuana, methamphetamine, heroin, and cocaine, as well as weapons. This special team has made more than a hundred felony arrests for narcotics and/or illegal weapons possession and has seized more than $500,000 worth of drugs.

3. NERO

Nero came to the New Castle County (Delaware) Police Department from Budapest, Hungary, as part of an exchange program between U.S. and Hungarian law enforcement agencies. His partner, Officer Phillip Aufiero, recalls that he first met the energetic and alert German shepherd when Nero was eighteen months old and "only understood Hungarian, and I had to learn those commands." It was not long before

Nero understood English and the two partners were inseparable. Throughout his career, Nero received countless commendations for bravery. He was responsible for finding more than $1 million worth of illicit drugs, missing cash, and lost property. He was credited with finding several lost children and Alzheimer's patients and he saved his partner's life: When a robber pulled a gun and tried to shoot Officer Aufiero, Nero sprang into action and knocked the pistol out of the robber's hand. In the late 1990s, Nero was given a "desk job" serving as a police representative at community events and in neighborhood schools. Nero died in September 2000, and he is remembered by his department and his community as "Nero the Hero."

4. ANDO

Officer Jim Davison was Ando's partner in LaGrange, Georgia. Ando was trained in patrol and narcotics detection. The Officer Davison-K-9 Ando team helped the Georgia Criminal Investigations Division and the Special Investigations Unit apprehend several wanted criminals, including two murderers, four bank robbers, and one of the U.S. Marshall's most wanted fugitives. Ando was killed the day after Christmas in 2000 while he was pursuing a drug suspect through a heavily wooded area. Ando had gone into the woods twice in search of the man; on his third trip, he went farther into the dense forest and did not return. He was found drowned in a creek. The suspect, captured two days later, had multiple dog bites and scratches on his arms and legs. Officer Davison and his fellow police officers remember their brave colleague, Ando, who gave his life trying to catch and hold onto a fleeing criminal and likely saving the lives of other officers.

5. **BODI**

A police dog with the Orange County (Virginia) Sheriff's Office, Bodi was shot and killed as he was pursuing an escaping suspect. Bodi was the first police dog (and the first animal) to have his life and contributions recognized in a memorial resolution by the Virginia General Assembly. His partner, Lieutenant Tim Murphy, noted that human police officers receive commendations all the time, but it is unusual for communities to recognize the heroism of canine police.

6. **L. C.**

All we know about L. C. is that he was a police dog in Wasilla, Alaska, who was shot in the line of duty in 1998 in Fairbanks. What happened as a result of L.C.'s death serves as a model of community action. Service clubs and community volunteers went into action to recognize and protect their canine police. The Lions Club purchased specially made bulletproof vests for the police dogs at a cost of $1,200 each in the belief that it was a small price to pay to keep the dogs safe. Perhaps L. C.'s replacement, Hero, can live up to his name without giving up his life.

7. **SEVO**

When Sevo and his partner, Officer Scott Gilchrist, of the Topeka (Kansas) Police Department, stopped a suspicious-looking person on New Year's Eve in 1998, they were both alert and anticipating trouble. They were so right. The suspect first tried to run, but when he was pursued, he suddenly turned and rushed Officer Gilchrist with a knife. Sevo jumped in front of his partner, taking the knife in his chest. Sevo kept on fighting to protect Officer Gilchrist, who was able to

subdue the suspect and then rush Sevo to the emergency veterinary clinic. Unfortunately, the multiple
knife wounds and loss of blood cost Sevo his life—
another valiant police dog who died protecting others.

8. LUKE

Luke and his partner, Sergeant David Dubiel, work
with the West Hartford (Connecticut) Police
Department. In 2002, they received Connecticut's
most prestigious award for K-9 teams—the Daniel
Wasson Memorial K-9 Award for bravery and outstanding police work. During their partnership,
Sergeant Dubiel and Luke have worked with the
Connecticut State Police and the East Hartford Police
to track and arrest two men who fled the scene of a
serious car accident, tracked and rescued a citizen
taken at gunpoint after shots had been fired in a dis-
turbance, apprehended a fleeing suspect in a burglary
in progress, and arrested suspects in a car highjack-
ing. Among fellow West Hartford officers, Luke is
known as a relentless tracker and a devoted partner.

9. CHARLIE

In the words of a September 24, 1999 USA Today arti-
cle, "In the world of explosives-detecting canines,
there is good, there is very good, and then there is
Charlie." Charlie, a black Labrador retriever who was
originally bred to be a guide dog for the blind and disabled, but he was a guide dog school dropout. His
problem was his nose—he could not resist all the great
smells around him. His sniffing turned out to be his
greatest asset, and Charlie became top bomb detector
for the Bureau of Alcohol, Tobacco, and Firearms
(ATF). In his five years with ATF, Charlie found two
hundred illegal guns and five hundred pounds of

explosives. Perhaps his most remarkable find, a favorite story of his partner, ATF Agent Grace Sours, was a 130-pound cannonball buried in a field near a Civil War battlefield. Sours says, "That means he tracked the scent of [gun]powder from the middle of the [1800s]." When Agent Sours was promoted and reassigned, Charlie took early retirement, but his influence continues to be reflected in the expanded use of scenting dogs. Local, state, and federal law enforcement agencies report using more than three thousand dogs to help locate drugs, weapons, and bombs. Airport and building security police routinely use dog partners, as do those in the Pentagon, the Central Intelligence Agency, the Internal Revenue Service, and the U.S. Department of Agriculture. Thanks, Charlie![1]

10. SIRIUS

Last, but not least, are the indefatigable canines who worked at the World Trade Center and the Pentagon following the tragedies of September 11, 2001. Sirius, a true representative of all those hard-working pups, was killed when one of the towers collapsed. We remember Sirius and his fellow working dogs, along with all of the police officers, firefighters, and innocent civilians who were injured or died.

Note: There are organizations that raise funds to help purchase bulletproof vests for police dogs. Two of those groups are Vest-A-Dog (www. dogvest.com) and Pennies to Protect Police Dogs (www.penniestoprotectpolicedogs.org).

Dogs in War

Dogs and human beings have shared a special, and sometimes puzzling, relationship for centuries. What we do know about the evolution of the human-canine connection makes a fascinating tale about partnership, love, conflict, and betrayal. Here are ten pieces of the story that demonstrate both the wonder and the occasional awfulness of one aspect of our relationship—wartime.

1. THE EARLY YEARS

From the earliest times, dogs have been by our side in peace and in war. In wartime, they have saved countless lives, often sacrificing their own. They have shown bravery under fire and brought comfort to the injured and dying. On our own continent, we have evidence from as far back as four thousand years ago of dogs and Native Americans living, working, and fighting together. The dogs were companions, hunters and fishers, pack animals, sentries, and attack dogs. During Roman times (27 BCE–395 CE), armies used formations of dogs wearing armor and spiked collars to charge into battle against their enemies. In the fifth century CE, Attila the Hun used giant Molossians (predecessors of the mastiff) and Talbots (predecessors of the bloodhound) in battle. During the Middle Ages (476 CE–1453 CE), dogs were used to defend caravans and to fight in battle. Sixteenth-century Spaniards used dogs to help them conquer the Indians of Mexico and Peru. From the early 1300s to 1770, the French Navy used trained attack dogs to guard their docks. (Their use ended in 1770, when a young naval officer was killed by one of the dogs.) By the 1700s, dogs were employed less as warriors and more as sentries. In the Seven Years War (1756–1763), Frederick the Great's Prussian army engaged dogs' skills as messengers between headquarters and the front lines. By the late 1700s, Napoleon had sentry dogs traveling with his armies to warn the troops of possible attacks.

2. FROM THE 1800S TO THE WORLD WARS

By the time of the Seminole War in Florida (1835), dogs regularly accompanied soldiers. The American Canine Corps was formed that same year to recruit and train dogs for roles as sentries, scouts, and messengers. In Florida and Louisiana, trackers use bloodhounds during the 1840s to find Indians and runaway slaves in the swamps. During the Civil War (1861–1865), dogs were critical as messengers, guards, and unit mascots. Over the next few decades, dogs became a part of most military ventures. In 1884, the German Army established a military school to train war dogs. Dogs were scouts in the Cuban jungles during the Spanish-American war (1898) and "ambulance dogs" in the Russo-Japanese War of 1904–1905. (The Russians trained these dogs to accompany ambulances and guard medical personnel and injured soldiers.)

3. **WORLD WARS I AND II**

Dogs continued to serve as sentries, messengers, and mascots during World War I (1914–1919). It was during World War II (1939–1945) that their roles expanded beyond any expectations. After the Japanese attack on Pearl Harbor, the U.S. Army Quartermaster Corps established the War Dog Program. The American Kennel Club and a group called Dogs for Defense mustered dog owners across the country, calling for donations of well-trained, intelligent dogs to be specially trained to serve as guards at civilian war plants. It was not long before the demand for sentry dogs was greater than the estimated need. By late 1942, the program had expanded to include training of dogs for the Navy and the Coast Guard as well.

4. **WAR DOG TRAINING**

Although dogs had been serving in battle for centuries, the wars of the twentieth century demanded new kinds of training. The Quartermaster Corps set up five permanent training centers and two temporary ones and even developed a training manual, *TM 10-396, War Dogs* (July 1, 1943). With the exception of sled dogs, which had been used for decades on snowbound battlefields, dog induction and training was new for the Army. During the dogs' basic training, they learned basic obedience (heel, sit, stay, and come commands) and became accustomed to muzzles, gas masks, military vehicles, and gunfire. Then, the specialized training began.

War Dog Reception and Training Centers were located at Front Royal, Virginia; Fort Robinson, Nebraska; Cat Island, Gulfport, Mississippi; Camp Rimini in Helena, Montana; and San

Carlos, California. Temporary training centers to train mine detection dogs were located at Beltsville, Maryland, and Fort Belvoir, Virginia. The mine dog training was eventually transferred to San Carlos.

5. SPECIAL TRAINING

Four training regimes prepared 10,425 dogs for their special war duties in World War II. *Sentry dogs* were trained to work in the dark, when surprise attack is most likely. The sentries worked on a short leash and learned to warn their human partners by growling, assuming an alert stance, or barking. More than nine thousand dogs were trained as sentries for costal fortifications, harbors, arsenals and ammunition dumps, airfields, depots, industrial plants, and beach patrols for enemy submarines. *Scout dogs* learned the same skills as the sentry dogs, but they were trained to work in silence so they could detect and warn of snipers, ambushes, or the presence of enemy soldiers. Scout dogs could detect the presence of an enemy up to a thousand yards away, long before their human partners knew anyone was near. They were particularly effective in the dense jungles of the Pacific islands. More than four hundred scout dogs served overseas. *Messenger dogs* had to be extremely loyal and able to work with two handlers. These dogs learned to travel silently and to identify potential dangers, such as snipers, booby traps, and bombs, and use natural cover on their missions. One hundred fifty-one messenger dogs were trained during the war. *Mine dogs* were trained to detect trip wires, booby traps, and land mines (metallic and nonmetallic). Some 140 mine dogs were trained. Those deployed served in North Africa with mixed success because the dogs had difficulty finding mines under combat conditions.

6. RECOGNITION OF SERVICE BY WAR DOGS

Many of the ten thousand-plus World War II dogs had outstanding service records. Some were awarded combat medals; however, the medals were revoked later because Army policy did not allow decorations to animals. Objection to the policy prompted the War Department to allow publication of commendations in the General Orders of individual units. Approval eventually was granted to issue citation certificates to the donors of war dogs with exemplary performance records. The oldest U.S. memorial to war dogs, dedicated in 1922, is in the Hartsdale (New York) Pet Cemetery. A World War II memorial was dedicated many years later, in 1994, at the U.S. Marine Corps War Dog Cemetery on Guam, honoring the dogs who served in the Pacific.

7. OUTSTANDING WAR DOGS

Two World War II dogs gained wide attention, Chips and Dick. Chips, later the subject of a Disney movie (*Chips the War Dog*, produced in 1993), was donated by Edward Wren of Pleasantville, New York. Chips was trained at Front Royal, Virginia, in 1942 and was one of the first dogs to go overseas. A sentry dog, he served with the Third Infantry Division in North Africa, Sicily, Italy, France, and Germany. The story that made Chips famous was reported by soldiers from Company I, Thirtieth Infantry Regiment. It seems that Chips broke away from his handler on a mission in Sicily and attacked a pillbox that contained an enemy machine gun crew. He held one enemy soldier by the arm and intimidated the entire crew into surrendering. Other stories credit Chips with the capture of several enemy soldiers by alerting others to their presence.

Chips was awarded the Silver Star and the Purple Heart, both of which the Army took back.

Perhaps not as well known as Chips but equally brave, Dick was donated by Edward Zan of New York City. He served with the Marine Corps in the Pacific, where he discovered a camouflaged Japanese bivouac and enabled a surprise attack by the Marines that resulted in annihilation of the enemy without a single U.S. casualty.

8. AFTER THE WAR

At the end of World War II, the war dogs were "reprocessed" so they could return to their families. The dogs were retrained to react to all people as "friendlies," and they were tested for reactions to people on bicycles and to the usual noises of civilian life, for example, doors slamming, radios and televisions playing, car horns honking, and motorcycles backfiring. Each dog also received a veterinary checkup before going home. Some previous owners did not want their dogs back so, with the help of Dogs for Defense, these pups were sold to new owners. By early 1947, all the returning war dogs had come home.

9. DOGS IN KOREA AND VIETNAM

Dogs have continued to serve in the armed forces, in both war and peace. American troops in Germany have used sentry dogs since the end of World War II. About fifteen hundred sentry dogs served in the Korean War (1950–1953), after which the sentries continued to relieve manpower shortages by guarding airfields and equipment storage areas. During the Vietnam War (1961–1975), about four thousand dogs were trained and used as sentries and scouts and as mine dogs to sniff out booby traps, land mines, and the enemy hiding in tunnels or under water. Two hundred eighty-one of the four thousand were killed in action; most of the rest, unlike their human partners, did not come home. They were either put to sleep or left behind to an uncertain fate.

10. LATE TWENTIETH-CENTURY WAR DOGS

Since the Vietnam War, the use of dogs in war has persisted. In 1988, the Israelis trained rottweilers to carry bombs into Lebanon on suicide missions. In 1989, when the Berlin Wall was torn down, East Germans used dogs to patrol the border as well as to serve as watch/attack dogs. During the Persian Gulf War in 1991, the French used more than a thousand German shepherds to protect soldiers and equipment, and the U.S. had eighty-eight guard dog-handler teams. To honor those American dogs who have served and continue to serve their country, the U.S. Postal Service is considering a petition for a stamp for military dogs.

HONORABLE MENTION:

Budda is a representative of the approximately thirty-five hundred Vietnam war dogs euthanized or left behind. He first saw combat with his partner, Sergeant Bob Brown, in mid-1966 as a mine and grenade dog. Budda was very effective at his job and unusually tolerant of the constant changes of place and activity that were part of the Vietnam soldier's life. In 1967, Budda and Sergeant Brown ("Brownie") were chosen for a secret mission with the Fifth Special Forces' A Team. After that mission, "Brownie" was reassigned to the States, but Budda had the hardest adjustment of all. He continued to be an outstanding scout dog, but his attitude was never the same; he never got over losing his first handler and friend. However, Budda was a soldier and he continued on. He was there for hand-to-hand fighting in Kontum Province and for patrolling supply routes in 1968-1969. After five years of combat duty, Budda was retired to the kennels, but remained in Vietnam. Budda never came home, but he was luckier than many of the war dogs—in 1971, he was euthanized.

> *Pups for Peace: Since the March 27, 2002, Passover massacre that killed ten people and injured 172 more in Netanya, Israel, the organization, Pups for Peace, was created. Trained explosive-detection dogs have been deployed to Israel to fight terrorism. Labradors, German shepherds, and Belgian Malinois are the breeds of choice for the organization, which uses the dogs to check bus stops, shopping malls, cafés, and any other possible suicide bombing targets in the volatile Middle East. For more information about the dogs, organization or how you might help, contact: www.pupsforpeace.org.*

War Dog Memorials

With the establishment of these memorials, the dogs of war are no longer "orphans" of the army. Today, we celebrate and remember their acts of courage, loyalty, and ultimate sacrifice from the American Revolution through the world wars, the Korean and Vietnam wars, to the wars in the Persian Gulf and Iraq.

Prince was just one of so many dogs that served in the war. He didn't earn medals or make the cover of *Time*. He went to the Vietnam War and did the job he was trained to do. But the story of Prince and his handler, Wayne Cross, illustrates how important our dogs were in saving lives.

As told by Cross:

> I was assigned to work Prince in the Arizona Territory with the Fifth Marine Regiment. We had worked a twenty-five-day commitment seven months earlier and had some success with booby traps. Hotel Company was running patrols off of Liberty Bridge into the Arizona Territory and had been tripping a lot of booby traps. The Company Commander remembered how good

Prince had been with booby traps and requested that we be assigned to help them with the booby traps.

The mines were in a hole about eighteen inches deep with the explosives buried in the side of the hole and a trip wire used to detonate. The hole was then covered and camouflaged to blend in with the ground. When we patrolled down the river the next morning, Prince located a booby trap set up across the trail. It was an old grenade with a wire attached to the pin and across the path to a bush. The squad detonated it in place. About two hours later in the patrol, Prince alerted by sitting down. This was his alert for a booby trap. The trail was clear with no bushes or trees. It was just a clear area. I reported it to the squad leader and proceeded forward. I was gingerly pushing my boot in front of me looking for a hole. I found a cloth covering a hole. I backed off and advised the squad that I believed we had a box mine. I had never encountered a booby trap like this before. It turned out to be a U.S. 105 round buried in the side of the hole. I could only imagine what damage would have been done if a Marine had stepped onto that hole.

In the next few days, Cross and Prince would work relentlessly, despite the Cross's repeated requests that his dog needed a break. With the death of several more Marines who had stepped on box mines (without the presence of Prince), Cross was ordered to keep going. Prince was greatly needed, but he was exhausted. The following morning began just as before:

We had been patrolling for about six hours and Prince was very tired. It was so hot. As we walked I saw him move to his right about a foot and then move back to his left. He had just walked around a spot in the path. I saw all of this and should have recognized it as an alert by a very tired dog. He let me know that there was something right in front of me. I, too, was exhausted and it did not register in my brain. I continued to walk and felt the ground give way about the box mine. I felt my foot fall into the hole and knew immediately that I was going to die. I felt my foot hit the trip wire and braced for the explosion. I heard a pop and saw a small white cloud of smoke drift up in front of my eyes. A dud! At first I was angry with Prince for not doing his normal alert, but I remembered what I was taught in dog school. Dogs will alert in many different ways. A good handler will recognize the alerts as they come or he won't survive. Prince alerted, but I was too tired to see it. He was looking at me like, "Why did you do that? I told you something was there."

Only one patrol a day went out after that incident. While we were there, no one was ever wounded or killed while Prince was walking point. I watched Prince a lot closer after that and became a better handler.

1. War-Dog Memorial
   March Field Air Museum, March Air Force Base
   Riverside, California
   www.marchfield.org/wardog

2. Sacrifice Field (in front of National Infantry Museum)
   Fort Benning, Georgia
   www.war-dogs.com

3. War Dog Memorial in Guam—WWII
   In honor of the Dobermans who served with the Marines in 1944
   www.geocities.com/Heartland/Plains/7109/wardogs

4. U.S. War Dog Memorial
   The Vietnam Veterans Memorial
   Holmdel, New Jersey
   www.njvvmf.org

5. The Hartsdale Pet Cemetery—WWI
   75 N. Central Park Avenue
   Harstdale, New York
   (800) 375-5234
   www.petcem.com
6. Vietnam War Dogs
   Streamwood, Illinois
   www.wardogsmemorial.org/Dogs_Save.asp
7. Vietnam War Dogs
   Port Neches, Texas
   www.wardogsmemorial.org/Dogs_Save.asp
8. South Pacific
   South Pacific Ocean at Alexander Headland for
   Australian Tracker Dogs in South Vietnam.
   www.war-dogs.com/memorial_memories2.htm
9. National War Dog Memorial Fund
   c/o Vietnam Dog Handlers Association
   P.O. Box 5658
   Oceanside, CA 92052-5658
10. Honoring War Dogs
    Check the dogs who served in all the different
    armed services at:
    http://members.aol.com/veterans/warlib5d.htm

An Akita and the
O. J. Simpson Case

When the horrific details of the murders of Nicole Simpson and Ronald Goldman were released, a murmur was heard throughout the canine community. Animal behaviorists, dog trainers and breeders, and veterinarians were instantly suspicious about what really happened. For anyone who knows the Akita breed, it was difficult to believe that Nicole Simpson's Akita, Kato, would allow anyone to savagely attack her and do nothing.

1. BEFORE THE MURDER

Kato lived a life not so different from that of many children of divorced parents. He moved back and forth between Nicole Simpson and O. J. Simpson's homes, along with the children. Although the Simpsons had clearly divided households, Kato still viewed O. J. as the alpha male and Nicole as the alpha female—important roles in the canine world.

2. THE CONDITION OF KATO (PHYSICALLY)

According to Akita breeders around the nation and animal behaviorists, the mere fact that Kato was in perfect condition is proof that the dog knew Nicole Simpson and Ronald Goldman's murderers. "He would have had blood, stab wounds, maybe he would have been killed himself," says Chris Clecak of Mariah Akitas in Indianapolis, Indiana. "No Akita would have simply allowed his mistress and friend to be slaughtered and do nothing."

The Akita is a Japanese fighting dog known around the canine world to be very aggressive when protecting his property or people. It is said that this breed in particular would willingly die to save his mistress or master.

"These dogs are so family-oriented and protective," says Cathy Spurlock of Mikoni Akitas in Midlothian, Texas, "an Akita will often stop family members from play wrestling by stepping in between."

"Only a dominant alpha [human] leader would have prevented an Akita from protecting his own family," says Clecak.

3. THE CONDITION OF KATO (EMOTIONALLY)

The emotional condition of Kato is another story, and to most animal behaviorists and Akita breeders, it is a significant clue in the case. After the murder, neighbors reported strange howling from the normally quiet dog. This is particularly strange because Akitas are quiet animals. Many experts suggested that the anguished cry showed that Kato witnessed something horrible but was unable to stop it.

4. WHY AN AKITA WOULDN'T STOP THE MURDER

"One would assume," says Akita breeder Clecak, "if the dog knows the attacker and the attacker is a leader within the family, it wouldn't be his place to intervene. No matter how painful to watch." As the alpha female, Nicole Simpson was clearly the victim. Many Akita breeders have speculated that, given the tumultuous relationship between the Simpsons, Kato learned from an early age to stay out of the way. "Truly," says Spulock, "it's the only explanation if Kato was indeed a witness to the murders."

Almost a decade ago, actress Susan Cabot was murdered by her own son while their two Akitas were in the house. It was and is still believed that the dogs did not intervene because the fight was between an alpha male and an alpha female. On the other hand, there are nearly three dozen documented cases of Akitas protecting their home/people against invaders, and each time the invader lost miserably, requiring anywhere from dozens to hundreds of stitches.[1]

"These are reasonable assumptions given the nature of the Akita," says Spurlock, "because the Akita has no fear."

5. THE POWER OF AN AKITA

Akitas can weight up to one hundred to one hundred twenty pounds. They are large, powerfully built animals used to fighting, hunting, and bringing down large prey. "When Bear—an Akita—was just eight months old, he chased down a wolf," says owner Jim Choate. The speed and agility of the Akita is awesome, and they are incredibly tenacious and brave animals. For centuries the Akita was used as a fighting dog, and the breed nearly became extinct. Unwilling to lose this treasured breed, the Japanese government finally stepped in and prohibited the bloody spectacles. The breed was later used for big game hunting, and they are known to be powerful swimmers, having saved many near-drowning victims.

In response to the argument that Kato was simply frightened by the attacker, most Akita breeders laugh. "Centuries ago, these dogs were bred to hunt and fight bears. They were built for punishment. Fending off a man is nothing for an Akita and I don't know one Akita that would back down from a fight." Clecak is not alone in this opinion. Akita breeders around the globe have speculated about why Kato would have simply watched the attack on his mistress, and all have agreed fear was not a reason.

"Let's put it this way," says Clecak, "if the attacker had been a stranger, he would have been shredded. Not hurt or injured, but killed by an Akita."

6. THE CHARACTER OF THE AKITA

The Japanese consider the breed to be a symbol of good health and good fortune. Today, they are strictly companion dogs. Akitas are extremely affectionate with children because they are loyal, patient, intelligent, and loving. They are also described by animal behaviorists and breeders as calm and dignified. Akitas are happiest when they are part of a pack with strong, loving alpha leaders. Respecting their alpha leaders is key to their happiness.

7. KATO DURING THE MURDER

O. J. Simpson's defenders initially speculated that Kato wasn't a witness to the murder, so all of the animal expert theories on the alpha male/alpha female didn't apply. But Kato had blood on his underbelly, leading most to believe that he lain over or near his mistress after the killer left. "With a conflict between the alpha male and female, that was really the only thing Kato could do. They are extremely loyal dogs. After he realized she was dead and couldn't be saved, I'm sure that's when he began to howl. Akitas mourn," says animal behaviorist Denna Johnson.

8. AFTER THE MURDER

After the murder, when Kato was returned to the O. J. Simpson homestead, his behavior was recorded before a national audience. While CNN and a local station captured footage, canine experts noted the dog's odd behavior. He sat in the middle of the driveway, aloof, and when Simpson arrived in his white Bronco, Kato did not greet him. According to Akita expert Barbara Bouyet, who witnessed the meeting between Kato and Simpson, "That dog looked into the car, stiffened, backed up, barked, and backed up again when he saw O. J." Bouyet noted that this kind of behavior is very uncharacteristic of an Akita and could only be explained by that person having done something very bad. And New York's *Newsday* included in a November 13, 1994, essay that Akita experts believe, "From the depths of his loyal, ruined heart, Kato [was saying to O. J.] 'You. You. It was you.'"[2]

9. WHERE KATO LIVES TODAY

Today, Kato lives with Simpson and his children (from his marriage to Nicole). It is a fact that many Simpson defenders claim is proof of his innocence. Over time, Kato appears to be a normal, healthy Akita.

Animals do not hold grudges. There is no evidence that Simpson ever harmed Kato. This is relevant because only if Kato were beaten by his alpha male or female would he display signs of submission or fear.

Animal behaviorists agree that it was not unusual for Kato to adjust over a period of time to life with Simpson after the murders, particularly if O. J. had already established himself as the alpha leader.

10. **KATO THE WITNESS**

"Would have, could have, should have . . ." is the response of animal trainers and behaviorists. Johnson, as do others, believes things might have played out much differently in the courtroom and for the jury had Simpson and Kato been separated after the murder. Had the meeting of man and dog been delayed until Simpson was in court, Kato's reaction would have been compelling. Had Kato eagerly greeted his master, that would have been points for the defense. But, many suspect, the most likely reaction would have been avoidance and nervousness. Since this landmark case, police departments and legal offices are now giving more credence to canine witnesses.[3]

(For more information about Akitas, log on to www.akitaclub.org or www.mariahakitas.com or contact breeder Cathy Spurlock by writing to Mikoni Akitas, 3831 Sudith, Midlothian, TX 76065.)

Additional Murder Canine-Witness Factoids

On December 24, 2003, a very pregnant Laci Peterson took her golden retriever, McKenzie, for a walk and disappeared. McKenzie was found dragging a muddy leash and was returned to his yard by a helpful neighbor. By that same evening a massive search for Peterson was in effect. Unlike the Akita, the notoriously friendly golden would allow a stranger to approach, sparking new debates among dog lovers. Once again, a dog was a key witness in a murder case.

Dogs in Court

While Kato, the dog, not the handyman, barely got a mention during the O. J. Simpson trials, dogs have had their day in court. Dogs have run the legal gamut from having no rights to having lawyers, from being a victim to standing accused. There are now practicing lawyers whose sole purpose is to defend or prosecute dogs (and their owners), with each group claiming to protect the rights of the innocent. Whatever the reasons, whatever the cases, dogs have had a dramatic impact in our courts.

1. DOGS ON THE BOOKS

Before the 1800s, there was no legal concept of rights for animals and no notion of criminal prosecution for any cruelty toward animals. Punishment—if any—was at the discretion of individual law enforcement agencies. Early anticruelty laws in the United States protected animals of commercial value, such as horses, cattle, sheep, or pigs, and they affected only those who might harm another person's animals, leaving owners to do what they pleased with their own animals.

By the 1860s, U.S. law was extended to additional animals, for example, giving more rights to cats and dogs. Although animals were still viewed as property, owners had to abide by restrictions addressing abuse and neglect. As time passed and we became more conscious of animal protection, individual states and localities began to legislate what constitutes cruelty to animals. Today, there is considerable variation among jurisdictions, but the United States is generally "animal friendly."

2. LONGEST ANIMAL CRUELTY SENTENCE

In 1999 in Sacramento, California, a former veterinary technician was sentenced to seven years in prison— said to be the longest animal cruelty sentence ever. Caesar Cerda was convicted of fighting and running a dogfighting circuit. Before his conviction, Cerda made up to $5,000 a month from betting on his fighting dogs.

3. DOG COATS

To the shock of many, as recently as the 1990s, it was discovered that the Burlington Coat Factory was selling a men's parka labeled, "Mongolian Dog Fur." Although Burlington Coat claimed that it believed it actually was selling coyote fur, it pledged $100,000 to the Humane Society of the United States in December 1998 in support of a campaign to ban the commercial sale of cat or dog fur. Of course, the company immediately pulled its "Mongolian Dog Fur" outerwear from the market.

4. THE MAULING OF SHAWN JONES

Dogs don't always fare well in court, nor do their human owners. In June 2001, a ten-year-old Richmond, California, boy named Shawn Jones decided to ride his brand new bike in his neighborhood, where he was attacked by three pit bulls. He was dragged into a nearby field and mauled. Chunks of flesh were torn away from his face and arms, and his fingers and both ears were ripped off. When the owner of the dogs, Benjamin Moore, discovered this heinous act, he left the still-breathing boy to hide his dogs in three different locations in Richmond. Moore never called 911 or attempted to assist the child in any way. Shawn Jones was airlifted to Children's Hospital in Oakland, where he was listed in critical condition for a month. Moore was arrested and charged with two minor misdemeanors. He posted the $50,000 bail and was freed pending trial. (Moore was arrested again while out on bail for possession of cocaine.) Today Moore is serving time in federal prison on drug charges, and the statute of limitations on the dog attack (a misdemeanor) has expired. Meanwhile, Shawn Jones continues to require surgery for his massive injuries.

5. WHIPPLE VS. MARJORIE KNOLLER AND ROBERT NOEL

In March 2002, legal history was made when a jury found dog owner Marjorie Knoller guilty of second-degree murder for the brutal killing of her neighbor, Diane Whipple. Whipple was brutally mauled—blood was sprayed four feet up the walls and extended thirty feet down the hallway of the apartment building complex—outside Whipple's own door by two presa canarios (fighting dogs originally from Spain's Canary Islands). Knoller's husband was also found guilty of involuntary manslaughter and owning a "mischievous" animal. To read more about this landmark case, check out www.dogbitelaw.com.

6. A DOG'S TESTIMONY

On September 22, 2000, the persistent barking of Casper, a shih tzu, awakened his owner, who saw a man standing in her bedroom doorway. As she tried to call 911, the intruder knocked the phone from her hand and attempted to rape her. When the phone rang, the man ran—but not before Casper took his own little bite out of crime, leaving hair on the man's trousers that would later be entered into evidence. This was the first time a dog's DNA had ever been presented at trial in California, and it stirred controversy. (In fact, canine DNA had only been used once before in the United States, in Washington state in 1998 in a double homicide.) But the Sima Valley judge ruled the evidence admissible, resulting in the conviction of twenty-four-year-old Soum Laykham for assault and attempted rape.

7. THE WILL

In 1931, a poodle named Toby inherited $15 million when his owner died. According to the *Guinness Book of Pet Records*, Toby was named the richest dog in America—but it would not last. While Toby's owner was alive, Toby lived like a prince: he slept on silk pillows and ate only the best—served to him on a silver platter by a butler. After his owner's death, however, the poodle slept in a simple wooden basket in the kitchen and was reduced to ordinary dog food. A huge debate was ignited over the will among the deceased's relatives, and just two years later Toby was put to sleep by the estate's executors.

8. DANGEROUS DOG ACT

Under the United Kingdom's Dangerous Dog Act of 1991, any dog deemed to be dangerous or threatening may be destroyed. So, when thirteen-year-old mixed breed Beth snarled at two elderly women, reportedly distressing them, a judge ordered that she be euthanized. On April 6, 2001, Beth appeared before the court to defend herself. When she took the stand, she was asked to open her mouth, revealing that she had no teeth. Beth was found not guilty.

9. THE SHOW DOG MURDERS

Contrary to the belief that only people who love dogs go to dog shows, it can be a nasty business driven by greed, power, and prestige. On the May 15, 1994, British journalist Ian Burrell of the *London Times* reported that nine show dogs had been poisoned, five fatally. The canine murders, the *Times* reported, appeared to have been carried out by rivals who had poisoned different dogs with rat poison, tranquilizers, and even hallucinogenic drugs. One of the victims was a champion puli who died from internal bleeding. Other victims were sprayed with dye, painted with nail polish, or had clumps of hair cut from their coats to disqualify them from competition. No one was ever caught for these horrible crimes of England's show dogs; in fact, a more common assault on show dog has been to use high-frequency alarms, inaudible to humans, to distract or disturb the dog in front of the judges. The movie, *Best in Show*, parodies this real-life drama in the show ring.

10. THE HIT

So successful was a drug-sniffing police dog in California that drug dealers issued a contract on its life, offering $15,000 to kill the dog and put an end to his amazing drug-sniffing abilities. Responsible for more than a hundred arrests, the dog had so angered local gangs that they were determined to end his career. They got their wish when someone killed the canine cop, prompting the U.S. Senate to pass the Federal Law Enforcement Animal Protection Act in May 1999, which establishes penalties for assaulting or killing animals serving law enforcement agencies.

Things the Dog Bite King Wants Dog Owners to Know

Attorney Kenneth Phillips, the leading national authority on dog-bite laws in the United States, has often been referred to as the "Dog Bite King." He has appeared in dozens of national magazines and on television news programs, including CNN's, regarding some of the most controversial dog bite/mauling cases of our time. Although always on the go, Phillips has made himself available through his Web site, offering free legal advice to dog owners or victims of dog bites and/or attacks. Meet the King at www.dogbiteking. com. In the meantime, read the ten things Phillips most wants you to know

1. If your dog has never bitten anyone, you may still have to pay compensation (medical costs, pain and suffering, lost income, etc.) to a dog bite victim. Most states have laws that make dog owners automatically liable for dog bites.
2. If your dog has bitten someone, you have to pay compensation, you might have to pay punitive damages, and you're not permitted to avoid any of these payments by filing for bankruptcy. You

are asking for serious trouble if you keep a dog who nips or bites people, because society, the government, and the insurance industry have gotten fed up with the 800,000 serious dog bite injuries each year in the United States, the thousand victims who enter emergency rooms every day, and the $1 billion in losses every year.

3. To avoid the consequences mentioned above, every dog owner needs to have homeowner's or renter's insurance, because such policies cover dog-inflicted injuries. If you are a renter, the cost of insurance should be factored into your decision to get a dog.

4. Check your homeowner's or renter's insurance policy to make sure that it doesn't contain an *exclusion* for dog-inflicted injuries. Don't do business with any insurance company that will not protect dog owners.

5. Don't allow anyone under the age of twelve to put his or her face near your dog's face. That includes your own children if you have not taught them how to be safe around dogs (don't move the food dish while the dog is eating, don't snatch one of the puppies from the mother, etc.).

6. Dog parks are dangerous places for dogs when irresponsible people bring aggressive dogs there. Keep track of your dog, the other dogs, and the other owners, and note the ones you need to avoid.

7. Whenever your dog is off your property, keep him on a leash. It might help you avoid a dogfight and prevent your dog from being run over by a car. It's also the law in many places. Violating a leash law usually makes you responsible for anything that happens as a result.

8. If your dog is injured or killed through the negligence of another person, you can usually collect only the purchase price of a replacement dog, even if you spent more than that on veterinary bills. Unbelievably, the law treats dogs like items of personal property: in most places, the law does not recognize sentimental value, the value of companionship, or the emotional distress of seeing your dog injured or killed.

9. If you own a dog whose breed is considered to be dangerous, be especially considerate, caring, and sympathetic to people who seem afraid of your pet. You should even consider muzzling your companion in public. The government, the insurance industry, and certain private groups, like landlords, are starting to restrict and even ban certain breeds because too many owners use the opposite psychology with people who fear their dogs.

10. If you adopt out your dog and you are aware of a behavioral problem, put it in writing and make the new owner sign it.

Must-Have Guidelines for Dog Parks

In the last decade, there has been a big boom in the popularity of dog parks. Owners are working longer hours and, in hopes of making up for a lack of dog/owner time, dog parks seem to offer the perfect solution for exercise, a social outlet, and an opportunity to talk to other dog owners. Because such parks are designated exclusively for dogs, there are no joggers, children, cyclists, or picnickers to worry about. Although there are no written laws or reported legal opinions on dog parks, attorneys, professional dog trainers, and animal behaviorists across the nation have very strong opinions about such parks. The Dog Bite King, attorney Kenneth Phillips, says these parks are a breeding ground for disaster.

For this reason, it is very important to have enforced behavior requirements. Establishing and adhering to rules ensures better safety for everyone involved—whether they have two legs or four.

1. RULES FOR THE PARK

Rules for the park should be in writing and should posted on a sign visible to anyone and everyone who comes into the park. This ensures that there is no confusion about the rules and no misunderstandings. The rules should be set by a board or body of park users who establish safety guidelines that all park users agree to follow.

2. FENCE

Proper fencing should be provided so dogs can neither escape under it or jump over it. To ensure maximum safety, it must be a secure, enclosed area where the dogs can play.

3. SECURITY GATE

Just as with the fencing, there needs to be a secure gate—possibly two—so dogs cannot slip past owners when new dogs enter the park. It's all fun and games until someone loses a dog.

4. NUMBER OF DOGS PER OWNER

Common sense should prevail. One owner should not and cannot handle more than two (or possibly three) dogs. Typically well-mannered, well-trained dogs can suddenly become difficult if not impossible to control when a dogfight breaks out. Most often, the well-mannered pooch is not to blame, but there is still great excitement. Owners need to gain control of their dogs quickly in emergency situations. For everyone's safety, park users need to limit the number of animals they bring into the park.

5. AGE REQUIREMENT

While parents are still at work, it may seem like a good idea to let an older child take the dog to the neighborhood dog park. This is unfair and dangerous. A child cannot be expected to make mature decisions about other dogs and how dogs behave with one another. Additionally, should something go wrong, an adult needs to be on hand in case a dog needs to be rushed to the vet. For everyone's safety, parks should require that owners be at least eighteen years old to enter the park.

6. NEIGHBORHOOD DOG

The neighborhood dog park should be for neighborhood dogs. There is always someone who will show up with two or three unneutered male dogs with aggressive tendencies. Often, these are the same people who have had to leave other parks because of constant dogfights and, in some cases, altercations with other dog owners. Also, nonresidents don't need to meet/get familiar with your dogs for security reasons. For this reason, dog parks should require dog owners to live in the neighborhood so people know each other and their dogs.

7. NO DOGS LEFT UNATTENDED

The dog park isn't a babysitting service; owners need to be present at all times. Should you attend a park in which dogs are running free without owner supervision, leave.

8. NO DOGS WITH CRIMINAL RECORDS

As mentioned in 6, dog owners may join new dog parks after they have been ousted from another park for fighting. No dogs with a record of biting/injuring other dogs or people should be allowed in the park. This is where it gets difficult because there are no written laws. Talk to the new owner, learn more about the dog, do a little investigating to keep your park safe.

9. DOGS ON LEAD

Dogs should be on lead while coming into and leaving the dog park. This rule ensures some control over the dogs as they come and go. Wild, gleeful celebrations often occur as dogs greet and depart from one another—the perfect opportunity for dogs to either escape from the park or begin a scuffle.

10. A BOARD OF DIRECTORS

A board or body of park users should have some kind of power to issue and enforce the rules of the park. This group of people should be responsible for handling complaints and/or violations. A list of contact names, telephone numbers, and e-mail addresses should be made available to parkgoers. Mayors and/or city or county boards of supervisors may be able to help in establishing dog park boards and giving them some enforcement powers.

Reasons Why Even Safety Guidelines May Not Work

It is likely only a matter of time before dog parks are obsolete. Lawyers argue that such parks are a breeding ground for lawsuits. There are issues of negligence liability, bites and injuries resulting from another dog, dog-on-human attacks, dog-on-dog attacks, lawsuits against local governments and individual citizens. The previous chapter suggested that all dog parks adhere to certain safety guidelines, but there are a number of reasons (ten to be exact) why even these precautions can't prevent disaster.

1. RULES OF THE PARK

Posting park rules is one thing, enforcing those rules is another. Without a full-time park attendant, it is virtually impossible to impose park rules on everyone who uses it—two- or four-legged. It only takes one out-of-control dog to create a very messy, potentially dangerous situation. Although local animal control officers can be called, they are often overworked and unable to follow up with repeat offenders.

2. FENCE AND GATE SECURITY

Again, without a park attendant, securing the park's entrance/exit to ensure there are no escape routes is difficult. One of the more common complaints is that dog owners—watching their own dogs—inadvertently allow other dogs to escape.

3. NUMBER OF DOGS PER OWNER

Although the vast majority of dog owners are responsible parkgoers, taking only one dog per person, there are those who will come with three or more. Dog walkers enjoy the luxury of a dog park—bringing in anywhere from five to ten dogs. Without an enforcement officer to stop this, the ratio of dogs to people can become unbalanced, brimming with all kinds of dangerous possibilities.

4. RESPONSIBLE OWNERS

One of the most frequently reported problems in dog parks is irresponsible owners. Dog owners who are completely clueless about how aggressive their dogs really are or don't care, who have never socialized their dogs, or who bring a bitch in season and/or an unneutered male are all too common at dog parks. Even after their dogs repeatedly attack other dogs, these owners continue to bring them to the park, convinced this is the way to cure the dogs of aggressive behavior. Even the most happy-go-lucky puppy can trigger a fight with an older, less tolerant dog. Unleashed, wildly happy dogs are an open invitation for dogfights.

5. DOGS WITH CRIMINAL RECORDS

A few owners persist in bringing their dogs to parks with full knowledge of the animal's aggressive behavior.

Whether they are intentionally allowing their dogs to pick fights with other dogs for sport, don't care about the potential danger, or truly do not understand the severity of their actions, the outcome is always bad. The biggest problem is unneutered males. Even the friendliest dog can be threatened under certain circumstances, but dogs with a fighting past are a particular threat. Each time a dog fights, he hones his skills and increases his inclination to fight. Dogs who tend to pick fights with other dogs may be wonderful with people; they can be good companions and family pets, but they should be kept away from other dogs. With dogs off-leash and no professional trainer to intervene, all dogs and humans in the park are at risk.

6. DOGS ON LEAD

Happy-go-lucky owners almost always arrive at the dog park with a leashless dog. They come with the best of intentions, full of hope for a fun day and the promise of good times. Then, the dog sees a squirrel, a cat, another dog . . . at best, the good time is ruined by a chase; at worst, an animal and/or person is hurt.

7. DOGFIGHT

Once a fight has occurred, then what? Usually the dogs are separated, but without a professional on hand, few if any dogs are reprimanded properly. It bears repeating that each and every fight that occurs reinforces that behavior for the dogs involved. Additionally, watching a dogfight can be very stressful for other dogs. Kids who fight in high school are immediately sent to a counselor for counseling (and punishment). Most dogs keep on playing—the perfect reinforcement for more fights.

8. NEGLIGENCE LIABILITY

Your dog is attacked. You reach in, desperate to save your dog, and are bitten by another dog who is clearly at fault for the vicious attack. What rights do you have? According to the Dog Bite King (see www.dog-biteking.com), "negligence" is doing something unreasonable. But, because it is not unreasonable that a dog should be off-leash at the dog park, it will be difficult for you to establish yourself as the victim and to make any claims for medical expenses resulting from the incident.

9. HEALTH ISSUES

Most dog parks depend on the owners to keep the park clean. Without a regular cleanup crew, parks can be unhealthy. Dogs can contract a variety of diseases, including worms, from untreated, infected animals who come to the park. The assumption has always been that only loving, caring dog owners invest the time and effort to take their (well-cared-for) dogs to the park. Not so. Weigh the health risks—your own and your dog's—before spending too much time at the dog park.

10. THE WILD WEST

Attorney Kenneth Phillips likens dog parks to the Wild West. It's an image that is quite accurate. The dog park is a land of anything goes: it promises an hour of great fun, but the long-term ramifications of the dog park are often not what owners want. Dog parks teach dogs to jump wildly on people, ignore the call of their owners, and, possibly, to fight. Dog trainers insist that the same kind of fun and exercise can be had by hiking/walking/jogging with your dog and going through the paces of basic obedience.

Everyday Dogs Turned Heroes

Whether purebred or mutt, mastiff or Chihuahua, your dog is your most loyal companion and determined protector. Inside every dog is a hero, waiting to be called to help. If you look at your canine couch potato or your shy, nervous pup and think that's a bit of an overstatement, read on and reconsider.

1. SOPHIE, THE DEAF PUPPY

In Galloway, Scotland, on March 17, 2002, five-year-old Georgia Peck fell into the nearby river and was swept away. Although she screamed, the fast-moving water carried her away too quickly for anyone inside the family home to help. That's when the family's six-month-old, deaf dalmatian puppy leapt into the water and swam to the little girl. Because the puppy was born deaf and with a severely deformed jawbone, some had suggested the dog be put to sleep. Despite her disabilities, her owner refused, saying she couldn't see putting a dog to sleep for these reasons—and how Sophie repaid everyone! Somehow she knew that Georgia was in trouble and instinctively went to her rescue.[1]

2. BLUE, THE ALLIGATOR FIGHTER

When eighty-four-year-old Ruth Gay fell and broke her nose and both shoulders, her two-year-old Australian blue heeler would not leave her side—until he saw an alligator. Although Gay was aware of large alligators in the canal behind the family home in Fort Myers, Florida, none had ever approached the house before. But on this July afternoon in 2001, with no one to assist her as she lay helpless, the alligator saw a perfect opportunity to feast. As the alligator approached Gay, Blue charged, attacking the it until it was forced to retreat. Blue was treated for more than thirty puncture wounds.[2]

3. SPARKLES SAVES THE DAY

When Bruce Cole was talking a late-night stroll with his seeing-eye dog, he never expected they would wind up in the emergency room. Just as the duo was stepping off a curb, Sparkles suddenly hit Cole, knocking him to the ground. A neighbor rushed out to find a car, half driven onto the curb on one side and Sparkles, unable to move, lying in the street. Pushing her owner out of the path of an oncoming, reckless driver, Sparkles took the full brunt of the car. Today, they can no longer take their long walks, and it is uncertain whether Sparkles will ever have full use of her back leg—a necessity for a guide dog. Says Cole, "I guess the bottom line on all of this is that she is my hero. My question is, why can't dogs live to be one hundred years old? They really should. They deserve to. It would only be right."[3]

4. ROCKY SAVES THE DAY

A convicted sex offender broke into the home of the Staples family of Hatboro, Pennsylvania, already having attempted to solicit sex from a teenage girl and steal an elderly man's car earlier that night. He snatched then eight-year-old Laura Staples from her bed, carried her silently down the stairs, and headed for the front door, only to be met by Rocky, a one hundred-pound Rhodesian ridgeback—a breed used for hunting lions in South Africa. The scuffle at the door allowed Laura to escape and run screaming to her parents' room. The family called the police while Rocky inflicted enough damage that police were able to follow a blood trail to the hiding intruder.

Since the attack, Rocky's owners found him a friend—a female ridgeback named Adrian, from the movie, *Rocky* (Adrian was Rocky's girlfriend). The intruder was convicted on eighteen of nineteen charges, including simple assault, indecent assault, and robbery.[4]

5. FAITHFUL COMPANION

Today, a small bronze statue at Shibuya Station in Japan commemorates the loyalty of a dog. Every day, an Akita named Hachiko walked with his owner, Dr. Ueno, to the train station as the doctor went to work. Each evening, Hachiko waited at the station for his master's return. Even after Dr. Ueno's death in 1925, Hachiko continued to wait for his master at the station until his own death nearly ten years later.[5]

6. DOSHA'S LUCKY DAY

Dosha, a pit bull mix, is a dog with an indomitable spirit. On April 15, 2003, Dosha was hit by a truck near her family's home. When the local police arrived on the scene, they found Dosha so badly injured they decided to shoot her in the head to put her out of her misery. She was then transported to the animal control

center and placed in a freezer, awaiting proper disposal. When a worker opened the freezer door more than
two hours later, Dosha was sitting up. Treated for
hypothermia, bruising from the truck, and the removal
of a bullet (that just missed her brain), the ten-month-
old puppy has recovered fully, with the exception of a
slight hearing loss in her right ear. Now, that's one
lucky, and tough, dog.[6]

7.   HOMEWARD BOUND

In 1979, a Labrador/boxer mix named Jimpa turned
up at his house in Pimpinio, Australia, after walking an
estimated two thousand miles (3,220 kilometers)
across the continent. Fourteen months earlier, Jimpa's
owner, Warren Dumesney, had moved with his dog to
work on a farm in Nyabing, Australia. Jimpa apparently had had enough of farm life and went back home—
negotiating an almost waterless trek across southern
Australia and demonstrating the perseverance and
dedication that earn our admiration.[7]

8.   ENDAL—PHYSICAL THERAPIST, MARRIAGE COUNSELOR, AND LIFESAVER!

While serving in the Royal Navy during the 1991 Gulf
War, Allen Parton was involved in an accident that left
him with severe memory loss and wheelchair bound.
Parton says he was extremely depressed, angry, and
rude—something his new yellow labrador, Endal,
would not tolerate. Insisting that Parton remain active,
Endal saved the man's marriage and his sanity after
years of self-pity, according to the war vet. Then, in
2001, it was payback time. While out on a stroll,
Parton saw a car headed straight for them and pushed
Endal out of the way just as the car hit his chair. Endal
immediately pushed Parton into a sitting position,

covered him with a blanket, brought him a cell phone, and began running back and forth between a nearby hotel and his master—barking the entire time. When help arrived, Endal insisted on riding in the ambulance with his owner, refusing to leave his side. For his outstanding actions, Endal was awarded the Gold Medal for Animal Gallantry and Devotion to Duty in England.[8]

9. HAVING HEART

On June 29, 1999, William Lee Harris suffered a heart attack in the kitchen as his family slept. Cosmo, a Jack Russell terrier, is credited with saving Harris's life by running up and down the halls, barking to awaken the rest of the family. As Harris began to heal, the two began walking as part of his rehabilitation. The determined Jack Russell made Harris stick to the workout program. One month after his first heart attack, the two set out for another walk, and Harris suffered a second heart attack. Immediately recognizing the signs, Cosmo began barking and running back and forth between his owner and the house until help was reached. Cosmo was inducted into the Iowa Animal Hall of Fame.

10. HERO

On the morning of September 11th, computer technician Omar Eduardo, found himself on the seventy-first floor of the World Trade Center with his seeing-eye dog when the tower was struck by an airplane. People were pushing and screaming, glass could be heard breaking, and the smoke was becoming unbearable. "Not having any sight, I knew I wouldn't be able to run down the stairs and through all the people. I was resigned to dying and decided to free Dorado to give him a change to escape. It wasn't fair that we should both die in that hell." Eduardo unclipped his leash, then gave the dog a final pet and a nudge with the order to go. The two were separated, and Dorado was swept away in the crowd. Then he was back again, fighting his way toward his owner, and they walked down seventy flights of stairs. "It was then that I knew for certain he loved me just as much as I loved him. He was pre-pared to die in the hope he might save my life."[9]

III
Breeds

Best Breeds for Kids

The most common mistake parents make when buying a family dog is choosing a dog that is cute or the right size rather than considering breed and temperament. When picking a breed or mix, it is important to consider the children who will be with the dog. Dogs should be solidly built—able to take roughhousing by children—and patient and gentle in nature. Although many breeds are good with children, the dogs listed here are those most often recommended by veterinarians, dog trainers, and animal behaviorists—professionals who handle dogs every day.

1. LABRADOR RETRIEVER

Members of the retriever family are the most sought-after dogs in the world for companionship. Their good reputation with small children and other animals is known around the world. This recommendation includes the golden retriever, curly- and flat-coated retrievers, and Chesapeake Bay retriever.

2. STANDARD SCHNAUZER AND 3. BEAGLE

Many breeds in the hound family are very good with children. They are good-natured and have a very positive outlook on life, but they can be quite stubborn. It is their stubbornness that makes them frustrating for children who want to teach their dogs to fetch or come. Getting a beagle to do something it doesn't want to do is a test of patience and persistence.

4. COLLIE FAMILY

This group includes the border collie, briard, and collie. These dogs are very docile with children and full of energy. They are very patient, but they will take charge of a situation that gets out of hand—key qualities in working with livestock and playing with a roomful of children.

5. GERMAN SHEPHERD

Like the collie family, the shepherd is very patient and tolerant of the rough play of children. These dogs are great protectors and loving family members.

6. JACK RUSSELL TERRIER AND 7. SPRINGER SPANIEL

Members of the spaniel family are extremely playful and friendly. The popularity of the cocker spaniel in the late 1970s and early 1980s caused a great deal of inbreeding by backyard breeders (nonprofessionals), and biting became a problem. But the springer spaniel never reached the popularity of the cocker, steering clear of the overbreeding problems. Despite all of this, spaniels have traditionally been wonderful family dogs. (Note: ears can be sensitive to pulling.)

8. MOUNTAIN DOGS

This category includes the Great Pyrenees, Saint
Bernard, Great Swiss mountain dog, and akbash.
These dogs are ferocious fighters in defending their
flock but are extremely patient, loving animals within
the family. Even today, many of these dogs are "put to
work" in the wintertime, pulling children on sleds for
hours on end.

9. WEIMARANER (AND OTHER GUNDOGS)

Like many hunting dogs, the Weimaraner can be will-
ful and stubborn but is a wonderful companion dog,
always ready to play or to cuddle for a good nap.

10. POODLE

It's always the surprise breed! Although teacup and toy
poodles are not recommended for children, the poodle
is a wonderful breed for them, particularly the standard poodle. The standard is the surprise watchdog of
the canine world—powerfully built, fearless, faithful,
and always ready for a romp.

Top Biters

According to U.S. Centers for Disease Control and Prevention (CDC), about 4.7 million Americans are bitten by dogs every year, with children under the age of five the most frequently bitten. The list of dogs that bite most often is complicated. There are a variety of reasons why a dog might bite—owners trying to break up a dogfight might be bitten mistakenly, rough play gone too far, a warning bite to a child who is hurting the dog, or an aggressive assault on a stranger. The CDC reports having a problem in assessing the accuracy of the dog-bite list: Most people do not report the bites (or aggression) of smaller family dogs. With that in mind, here is the list of the ten dogs most likely to bite.

1. **Chow Chow**
2. **Old English Sheepdog**
3. **Lhasa Apso**
4. **Toy Poodle**
5. **Cocker Spaniel**
6. **Rottweiler**
7. **Pit Bull**
8. **Dachshund**
9. **Pekingese**
10. **Giant Schnauzer**

Breeds with a "Bad Dog" Reputation

All of these dogs are extremely affectionate family pets and very good with children, assuming they come from sound breeding. But because of the "tough guy" reputation of these breeds, some people own these dogs because they want a tough animal. These owners fuel the negative image and encourage the backyard breeding that enhances uncharacteristic and unwanted behaviors, such as turning on family members.

1. **German Shepherd**
2. **Bulldog**
3. **Rottweiler**
4. **Doberman Pinscher**
5. **Boxer**
6. **Mastiff**
7. **Great Dane**
8. **American Staffordshire Terrier**
9. **American Pit Bull Terrier**
10. **Staffordshire Bull Terrier**

Bite Prevention Tips for Joggers

According to the Humane Society of the United States, dog bites are the number one health problem for children in the United States and the number one hazard reported by joggers. By respecting the space and property of dogs—territorial animals by nature—joggers can diminish the risk of being bitten.

1. RESPECT THE DOG'S SPACE

Steer clear of the dog's perceived property line. Cross the street well before you approach a dog to avoid any threatening movements. If the dog is fenced, never poke sticks through the fence or throw things into the dog's area.

2. THE STARE DOWN

Forget what you've read about staring down a dog. If you are jogging past a house and the dog comes out, tell him, "no," in a firm voice, move to the other side of the street, and continue (slowly) on. Do not lunge forward, as though you are trying to run away, and do not stand to confront the dog. Eye contact can be perceived as a threat and the dog might feel challenged. Stay calm and move on.

3. CHASING DOGS

Do not chase dogs or encourage them to chase you. Many joggers believe "chasing the dog off" establishes them as "lead dog" for the next encounter. Not so. An equally bad idea is running away from a barking dog. Even a playful, exuberant pup can misinterpret this move and chomp down on a jogger's hindquarters, as he would another pack member, just for fun! Walk, be calm, and get past the dog's territory before running again.

4. AVOID STRANGE DOGS

Never pet a dog without asking permission, even if the dog is on lead and in public. Always ask first. Never step onto the property of a strange dog, even if you're trying to retrieve a ball or if the dog appears to be friendly.

5. DON'T APPROACH AN INJURED DOG

Go get help. Never handle an injured dog alone. For this reason, it is good for children to understand that a seemingly healthy dog might have an ear infection or arthritis. Simply petting a dog could hurt enough to provoke a warning bite.

In the event that an animal is injured and needs to be taken to the hospital, elicit help from a professional. If this isn't possible, and the dog needs to be rushed to the hospital, gently wrap a cloth around either the dog's head, to prevent him from panicking and biting, or around your arm, to protect against possible bites.

6. RUNNING AND SCREAMING

Running and screaming, high-pitched noises, and quick movements near an already aroused animal will kick in every natural hunting instinct the dog has. To a dog who is already excited, you have signaled that "the game is on." For the nervous or frightened dog, this behavior will only agitate and confuse him, causing the dog to react by biting out of self-protection.

7. LET SLEEPING DOGS LIE

It's fun to lie on dogs while they are sleeping, but children must be taught to leave a dog alone while he is sleeping in a doghouse or crate, or even curled up on the kitchen floor. This includes dogs who are sleeping or sitting contently in a car. No matter how friendly a dog looks, joggers should keep on jogging. Don't stop or whistle to a cute puppy. Just keep on burning those calories.

8. RUNNING WITH YOUR OWN DOG

It's unfair, it's not right, but you are a target for other dogs when you are running with your own. No matter how well trained your dog, be sure he has a leash that can be reeled in at the sight of another dog. Again, slow the pace, calmly tell the other dog, "no," as he approaches, and get out of there. Do not allow your own pup to bark, growl, or leap at other dogs, and do not allow sniffing or socialization with a strange dog. This also teaches your dog that jogging time is for jogging.

9. THE DOGFIGHT

Never put your hand into the middle of a dog fight. Do not scream—that will only heighten the hysteria. If you can, get out the garden hose and squirt them or get a rake—something to separate the dogs but keep you out of the ruckus. For the most part, domesticated dogs have no interest in harming humans, but they will bite if someone gets in the way.

10. UNDERSTAND THE SIGNS OF AGGRESSION

A wagging tail does not always mean a dog is friendly. A low-wagging tail, stiff and wagging, may be a warning sign. A dropped head, ears laid flat, and stiff legs are signs of aggression. Of course, growling and showing teeth are big indicators. Do not challenge, do not run away, do not stare down. Stay calm and move slowly away from the dog. If you're attacked, drop and curl into a ball, protecting your face and neck. As impossible as it may seem, try not to scream or kick back.

Most Intelligent Breeds

Actually, this list is somewhat misleading. According to animal behaviorist Dr. Stanley Cohen, author of *The Intelligence of Dogs: A Guide to the Thoughts, Emotions, and Inner Lives of Our Canine Companions* (Bantam Books, 1995), the list is based on a dog's ability to understand new commands in fewer than five repetitions. Lovers of breeds not mentioned on this list always take exception, but obedience trainers and animal behaviorists universally accept it.

The dogs of the breeds listed below understand new commands in fewer than five repetitions and obey the first command given 95 percent of the time or better.

1. **Border Collie**
2. **Poodle**
3. **German Shepherd**
4. **Golden Retriever**
5. **Doberman Pinscher**
6. **Shetland Sheepdog**
7. **Labrador Retriever**
8. **Papillon**
9. **Rottweiler**
10. **Australian Cattle Dog**

Most Difficult Breeds to Train

To clarify, this list has been compiled by trainers as the breeds most difficult to train. These breeds understood a new command only after eighty to one hundred repetitions and obey the first command given to them just 25 percent of the time or worse.

1. **Shih Tzu**
2. **Basset Hound**
3. **Mastiff**
4. **Beagle**
5. **Pekingese**
6. **Bloodhound**
7. **Borzoi**
8. **Chow Chow**
9. **Bulldog**
10. **Basenji**

HONORABLE MENTION:

Afghan Hound

Most Popular Breeds Registered with the American Kennel Club

1. Labrador Retriever
2. Rottweiler
3. German Shepherd
4. Golden Retriever
5. Poodle
6. Beagle
7. Dachshund
8. Cocker Spaniel
9. Yorkshire Terrier
10. Shetland Sheepdog

Best Working Security/Guard Dogs

Ranking the dogs from most qualified to least, the breeds listed below are assessed according to their territorial sense, aggressiveness, size and strength, courage, and ability or willingness to counterattack.

1. Bullmastiff
2. Doberman Pinscher
3. Rottweiller
4. Komondor
5. Puli
6. Giant Schnauzer
7. German Shepherd
8. Rhodesian Ridgeback
9. Kuvasz
10. American Staffordshire Terrier[1]

Best Barking Watchdogs

The breeds listed are comprise highly enthusiastic and energetic dogs who have scored high in ability and willingness to bark (vigorously) at an intruder or something that does not seem right. All are territorial and ready to alert their packs or families; they are listed from the most alert to the least in watching their home or property.

1. Rottweiler
2. German Shepherd
3. Scottish Terrier
4. West Highland Terrier
5. Miniature Schnauzer
6. Yorkshire Terrier
7. Cairn Terrier
8. Chihuahua
9. Airedale
10. Poodle (Standard and Miniature)[1]

HONORABLE MENTIONS:

Dachshunds and Fox Terriers

Breeds Least Likely to Succeed as Watchdogs

Listed from the least likely to the most likely, these dogs are least likely to bark at intruders and defend property against intruders. Gentle in nature, these breeds typically stay calm and quiet and remain undisturbed by whatever might be going on around them. However, it should be noted that most of these dogs are very specialized and very good at what they do, whether hunting or herding; they just aren't that interested in protecting the family silverware.

1. Bloodhound
2. Newfoundland
3. Saint Bernard
4. Basset Hound
5. Bulldog
6. Old English Sheepdog
7. Clumber Spaniel
8. Irish Wolfhound
9. Scottish Deerhound
10. Siberian Husky and Alaskan Malamute (tie)[1]

Most Popular
Dog names

Male Puppies

1. Max
2. Jake
3. Buddy
4. Sam
5. Rocky
6. Buster
7. Cody
8. Duke
9. Jack
10. Harley[1]

Female Puppies

1. Maggie
2. Molly
3. Lady
4. Sadie
5. Lucy
6. Daisy
7. Ginger
8. Abby
9. Sandy
10. Katie[1]

Largest Breeds

Dogs are listed from smallest to largest of large breeds; they all tip the scale at more than one hundred pounds.

1. **Kuvasz**
2. **Irish Wolfhound**
3. **Komondor**
4. **Anatolian**
5. **Saint Bernard**
6. **Great Pyrenees**
7. **Great Dane**
8. **Great Swiss Mountain Dog**
9. **Newfoundland**
10. **Mastiff Family** (ranked from smallest to largest: Bullmastiff, Spanish Mastiff, Pyrenees Mastiff, Neapolitan and Mastiff)

Smallest Breeds

These breeds, all under ten pounds, are listed from largest to smallest.

1. **Affenpinscher**
2. **Maltese**
3. **Chihuahua**
4. **Toy Fox Terrier**
5. **Toy Terrier**
6. **Small Continental Spaniel**
7. **Chinese Crested Dog**
8. **Yorkshire Terrier**
9. **Teacup Poodle**
10. **Chinese Imperial Ch'In (the Sleeve Dog)**

The giant can weigh approximately fifteen pounds. The classic imperial weighs four to five pounds, the miniature is three to four pounds, and the sleeve dog weighs between one and two pounds.

Best Hunting Dogs

In grading hunting breeds, courage and aptitude to learn and how well the dog can cover the ground and follow verbal and physical commands are essential information to the hunter. This assessment also includes how the dogs retrieve and handle birds or pursue wounded game.

1. **Labrador Retriever**
2. **English Pointer**
3. **Catahoula**
4. **Irish Setter**
5. **German Short-Haired Pointer**
6. **English Setter**
7. **Golden Retriever**
8. **Chesapeake Bay Retriever**
9. **Brittany**
10. **Springer Spaniel**

In the United Kingdom, where pack hunting is far more popular than in the United States, members of the hound family such as beagles and English foxhounds are used.

Biggest Myths about the Notorious Pit Bull

Just the name, pit bull, strikes fear in the heart of many; it is synonymous with vicious attacks, brutal death, and blood sport. In truth, the pit bull can be one of the gentlest, most social dogs in the canine world.

1. PITS DON'T MAKE GOOD FAMILY PETS

We often hear people say that all pit bulls are aggressive and unpredictable toward people and other animals. Historically, pits have always been great family dogs. In the old "pit days," when many a pit bull was taken home after surviving another dogfight, the dog instantly resumed his role as child's companion, stock dog, and family pet. It may seem ironic, but many of the pits' fighting characteristics have made them good family, therapy, and performance/agility dogs.

2. PIT BULLS CAN'T BE TRUSTED WITH HUMANS

It is important to note that fighting is part of the pit's genetic makeup. Pits are historically bred to test themselves against larger and stronger animals and against

The notorious pit bull is actually a
very loving dog and great with children.

each other. It is their instinct to win each fight.
However, pits have always been keenly aware of the
difference between work (that is, fighting or holding a
bull) and behaving appropriately with an owner. They
like being with their owners and can tolerate lots of
human contact; they are affectionate, loving animals.
A responsible owner—one who is kind and compassionate—and proper breeding are key to having a
friendly and trustworthy pit.

3. IT'S HOW YOU RAISE THEM

It's been said over and over again: If you raise your pit
bull like a Labrador or poodle, your pit bull will be just
like a Lab. Many well-intentioned but ignorant owners
have gotten pit bulls convinced that their sweet puppies' temperaments would ultimately be shaped by
how they were raised. Unfortunately, these well-mean-

ing but ill-informed folks are being unfair to their puppies, to their neighbors, to every dog their puppy-turned-dog meets. By not knowing as much about their puppy's heritage as possible, they are setting these dogs up to become dog-aggressive, and they are preventing them from reaching their greatest potential. Pits are naturally aggressive toward other dogs, energetic, and need lots of exercise. A pit bull is a pit bull and must be respected as such.

4. PIT BULLS MUST BE KEPT AS ONLY DOGS

Pit bulls get along quite happily with nonaggressive, nondominant dogs. They should be spayed or neutered (same-sex dogs are much more likely to fight), and one dog should be older than the other so a clear leader of the pack may be established. Pit bulls should not be paired with another pit or any other dominant breed.

5. PIT BULLS HAVE LOCKING JAWS

The awe of the pit's strength leads to urban legends about dogs with locking jaws that exert twenty thousand pounds of pressure per inch. The pit's skull is wide and his muscles well developed, but the anatomy of the pit bull's jaw and skull is no different from that of any other breed. No mechanism exists that allows the jaw to lock into place.

6. ALL FIGHTING DOGS ARE PIT BULLS

The stout, square-jawed dog known as the pit bull is actually many different breeds, each with its own distinctive characteristics (see 10, below). Other breeds, including the mastiff, have a much longer history of fighting, dating back to the Roman Empire. The pit bull did not attain its popularity as a fighting dog until the seventeenth century.

7. ALL PIT BULL OWNERS ARE DRUG DEALERS, GANGSTERS, OR ARE INVOLVED IN DOGFIGHTING

Unfortunately for everyone, the criminal element may be the most visible segment of pit bull owners, but it is certainly not the most representative. Pit owners range from former presidents and movie stars, to authors and teachers, to lawyers and laborers. Besides having to deal with the drug dealer stereotype and breed-specific legislation, reputable pit bull owners have to be thick-skinned enough to ignore rude comments about their dogs. They also have to vigilant about keeping their dogs from harm—from getting into fights or from being stolen by thieves looking for dogs to use as fighters or "bait." Respectable pit bull owners love this breed for its happy and loving personality.

8. PIT BULLS AND STAFFORDSHIRE TERRIERS ARE THE SAME; THEY JUST HAVE DIFFERENT NAMES

Not so. American pit bulls are not registered with the American Kennel Club, the American Staffordshire terrier is. Why is the subject of heated debate among American pit bull and Staffie owners. Pit owners argue that breed regulation limits coloring, size, and body/head dimensions, while Staffie owners maintain that their dogs are pure and meet all the AKC regulations. The distinction between the two breeds is that the American Staffordshire was selectively bred from the British Staffordshire bull terrier and is heavier, bulkier, and taller than the pit bull, with a smooth, short coat.

9. PIT BULLS GO INSANE WHEN THEY SMELL BLOOD

The myth goes like this: A woman was standing in her kitchen, talking to her beloved pit bulls, when she cut her hand on a jagged aluminum can lid. The pit bull got one whiff of her blood and went wild, killing his mistress and ripping her to pieces. There is no documentation for this story, but there are dozens and dozens of reported incidents in which a pit bull saved a child from drowning, a house fire, or being struck by an oncoming car.

10. A PIT BY ANY OTHER NAME...

The history of the pit bull is rich—family dog, loyal companion, fighting dog, and stock dog—with many names that go with it. The top ten names for pit bulls are:

1. American Bull Terriers
2. American Staffordshire Terriers
3. Bull and Terriers
4. Half and Halfs
5. Old Family Dog (Ireland)
6. Pit Dogs
7. Pit Terriers
8. Rebel Terriers
9. Staffordshire Fighting Dogs
10. Yankee Terriers

Most Common Behavior Problems (and Quick Tips to Fix Them)

According to the National Dog Trainers Association and trainers around the nation, there are ten common behavior problems that most dog owners face at one time or another. Being alert to these potential problems is really half the battle. The key: act fast and save everyone a lot of time and trouble.

1. HOUSEBREAKING

Ranked as the most frustrating new puppy/owner experience is housebreaking. For a step-by-step breakdown on housebreaking, look for *Teaching Basic Obedience: Train the Owner, Train the Dog* by Alexandra Powe Allred (TFH Publications, 2000). In the meantime, be sure to crate your puppy when you cannot watch him and pick up the water when you are not around so that he can't constantly refuel. By putting your puppy on a tight schedule of food and water, exercise, and times to go outside to relieve himself, you will find the system that works for both of you. Be patient.

2. DESTRUCTIVE BEHAVIOR

Destructive behavior runs a close second to house-breaking in owner frustration with puppyhood. The number one rule for discouraging chewing is to provide toys. Make sure your puppy understands which items are his toys and which are not! Be sure to crate him when you cannot watch him. Remember, for the first six months of his life, he is teething and nothing is more soothing to painful gums than chewing on your shoes or wooden chairs. Be watchful.

3. JUMPING

Your dog will only learn as much as you teach him. From day one, make jumping up on people a no-no. No matter how tiny or cute he is, jumping should be off limits.

4. NIPPING

This is a common problem with young puppies. Nipping appears to be relatively harmless because puppies are so small and cute, but it can quickly turn into a larger problem if not corrected. Nipping can turn into a dominating act, such as mauling, that can cause various problems, including disobedience, stubbornness, and aggression.

5. BARKING

Just like many other puppy problems, this one seems harmless enough. It's cute to hear them when they first find their voices and bark at toys, shadows, or even us (in play). This can quickly turn into a way of getting or demanding attention. Be sure to teach your dog when it is and isn't appropriate to bark. Barking at other dogs, cars, and people is not cute! Barking on command or when he hears a strange noise in the night can be rewarded. Never allow nonstop barking.

6. RUNNING AWAY

This is perhaps one of the most frustrating behavior problems and the most obvious cry for basic obedience training. Some breeds are more prone to roaming than others, but you can and should still train your dog to come when called. Never, ever chase your dog once he's escaped—it can turn to a game. Instead, you must get him to come *to you!* Make sure he is exercised regularly and enroll him in a dog training class. For male dogs, neutering can be very helpful as well.

7. DIGGING

Most dogs dig out of boredom. By faithfully exercising your dog and providing lots of toys and bones in the back yard, you can minimize his desire to dig. Nonetheless, many breeds are born diggers. Terriers, for example, tunnel after vermin. For them, provide a digging area such as their own sandbox or soft-earthed area. Teach them that the specified area is their area—nowhere else. Bury treats in the sandbox to encourage digging in that area. In the meantime, fill other holes made with the dog's own feces. Since most dogs do not like to dig in feces, this is an easy way to discourage digging.

8. JUMPING ON FURNITURE

From the first day your puppy comes home, do not allow him to sit or sleep on furniture. If you set a hard-and-fast rule of *no furniture*, your puppy will learn not even to try. Many of us will hold our puppy and sit on the couch, thinking that, technically, the puppy is on us. The puppy only knows that he is on the couch, likes it, and will try for that again. If you're thinking, "too late," be sure to check out the *Teaching Basic Obedience: Train the Owner, Train the Dog*. It contains many tips on how to beat this bad habit.

9. PULLING ON THE LEASH

A well-exercised and -trained dog doesn't pull on the lead. It is as simple as that. Even if your puppy is only eight weeks old, you can begin a training regimen with him that will ensure a lifetime of joyful walking. It's never too late to start and, yes, an old dog can learn new tricks. Basic obedience and exercise are key!

10. DOG-ON-DOG AGGRESSION

For younger pups, never allow barking at other dogs while walking. Many small dog owners allow this because it is funny to watch small dogs "tell off" larger breeds. In truth, this is very dangerous. If you have an older dog that is already aggressive toward other dogs, finding a canine group training class may be the key. Again, information about handling behavioral problems can be found in a good dog-training book.

The AKC-Approved Good Citizen Test

In 1989, the AKC's Canine Good Citizen (CGC) Program was created as a way to reward well-behaved dogs. If you think you've got a good citizen, try these series of tests that require your dog to behave in a socially acceptable manner. Remember, even the best dogs may fail such a test in public situations. If your dog is not used to traffic, loud noises, other dogs, or rambunctious children, his behavior may be radically different. Instead of an arbitrary and artificial test, here are ten questions you can ask yourself to determine how good your canine citizen is. When you are ready, log on to www.akc.org/love/cgc to learn more about the AKC and how you and your dog can earn an official CGC Award.

1. **IS YOUR DOG WELL GROOMED, HEALTHY, AND UP-TO-DATE ON ALL HIS REQUIRED SHOTS?**

This also means being up-to-date on his license. By taking your dog to the vet frequently, you also ensure that different people can handle him.

Author's Collection

An obedience-school graduate celebrates.

2. **CAN HE WALK ON A LOOSE LEAD (ON YOUR LEFT SIDE, COMMON PRACTICE IN BASIC OBEDIENCE AND SHOW TRAINING)?**

Holding a leash so taut that your dog is practically choking does not count as heeling. He should be able to walk happily and easily beside you without pulling on the lead.

3. **WALKING THROUGH A CROWD**

Your dog should be able to stay comfortably by your side and move in and out of crowds without fear, aggression, or agitation. His confidence should come from walking with you.

4. WHEN A STRANGER APPROACHES

Should a stranger approach while you and your dog are walking, your dog should be comfortable and confident enough to allow himself to be petted.

5. SIT, STAY, AND DOWN COMMANDS

Good citizens need to be able to sit and go down on command without resisting. Ask any dog trainer and he or she will tell you that the basis for all training is a solid "stay" command. Your dog should be able to sit and stay at command while other dogs walk by or a leaf blows past. This is a test in self-control.

6. RECALL

When you call your dog, does he come to you?

Author's Collection

A Good Citizen is able to obey commands and
remain calm in the presence of other dogs.

7. BARKING DOGS

Does your dog bark at other dogs when you go for a walk? It is important that you be able to walk comfortably without confrontations.

8. SOCIALIZATION

Is your dog socialized properly? Many dogs panic when they are confronted with something new. A ceiling fan, a person on crutches, or a man wearing an unusual hat can cause panic, barking, and/or flight.

9. HOW DOES HE REACT?

When your dog is exposed to something new and perhaps frightening, can he sit/stay on command?

10. ON BEING ALONE

When you leave your dog alone, is he responsible and able to control himself, or are your furniture and personal belongings fair game?

Teaching Your Puppy Tricks

By teaching your dog a variety of tricks, you can help him to learn more easily, and he will learn to work for praise. This will help training later, when you begin to teach basic obedience. Remember, this should be fun!

1. GIVE A KISS

Every time your puppy kisses you, say, "Give me a kiss." Social pups love to kiss, so this will be easy. The second he gives a kiss, praise him with hugs and verbal rewards. Keep doing it, and your dog will learn the phrase and will oblige on command. It will also teach him to kiss on command only, so there won't be constant slobbering.

2. FIND THE BALL

Armed with tennis balls, tell you dog to sit and stay. Then, show him the ball but do not allow him to leave his seated position. Place the ball several feet in front of him and instruct him to get the ball. When he does, reward him with play. As he learns the phrase, "Find the ball," move the ball further and further away. As soon as he begins to master the phrase, begin to hide the ball. Make the hiding places very easy, making sure he doesn't get frustrated. Spend several days in each new area where you hide the ball. Eventually, he will learn to sniff out the ball for himself. This teaches him to use all his senses—a trick that always makes dogs happy.

3. HIDE-AND-SEEK

Using the same principal as "Find the Ball," have your dog sit and stay. Move around the corner and call him. As soon as he comes he will find you. This not only teaches him to come when called, but it also begins the process of searching for you. Don't rush the trick; move a little farther away each day, making you a little more difficult to find. If your dog gets frustrated, move to an easier location until he builds his confidence.

4. SHAKE HANDS

Choose the expression you like: "How do you do?" "Shake hands." "Give me your paw." Place your dog in a sit position and have him stay. Then, standing in front of him, extend your right hand and say, "How do you do?" (or whatever you want to say). Repeat this over and over. It may take two days; it may take two weeks—be patient. Each time, have the dog sit, say the phrase, and extend your hand. Each time, end with reaching down and taking his paw so he knows what you are asking. Eventually, he will offer his paw in hopes of a reward or praise.

5. HIGH FIVE

The "high five" is a very easy trick for dogs who paw a lot. Just as you did with the "Shake hands," repeat the phrase, "high five," over and over. Each time, hold your hand a little higher so your dog has to "high five" a little higher. With continued practice, your dog can and will learn the distinction between "high five" and "shake."

6. BANG! BANG!

This trick will also ensure that your dog knows the "down" command. Each time you tell him, "down," cock your finger and shoot, saying, "bang!" After several down commands in a row, using the same tone of voice, say, "Bang!" Perform this trick over and over again. Eventually, he will learn the verbal ("Bang!") and physical (shooting motion) commands.

7. GET THE PAPER

When your dog is older and it's raining outside, you will love this trick. Whether you use the phrase, "Take it," or "Get the paper," you can teach Fido to fetch the morning paper. This is a slow building process that is great fun for your dog. As soon as your puppy is able to walk on a lead, go out to get the morning paper or mail. He might trip and stumble over the paper, but as he gets bigger and stronger, he will be used to handling it. Repeat "get the paper!" over and over as your dog carries the paper back to the house. If he drops it a dozen times, stop and give it back to him a dozen times. Eventually, the two of you will make it back to the house without incident and with the paper.

When you get inside the house, tell him, "Drop it" or "Release." Give him big praise when the job is done. Remember, it may be a year before you can actually let him trail his lead to retrieve the paper. Patience, patience!

A Labrador learning to fetch. This trick
can be fun for you and your dog.

8. HOLD IT!

With your dog in a seated/stay position, balance a bis-
cuit on his nose. As you begin this, let your hand hover
over the treat so you can grab the treat before he does.
Tell him to stay and say, "Hold it," while you keep the
treat on his nose. Only ask him to stay for a few seconds. Give him the treat and big hugs. Each time, tell
him, "Hold it," a little longer, teaching him patience
and self-control. He will learn that you will give him the
treat, but he has to wait for your command, "Okay!"
before he can eat it. Kids love this trick. And, again,
this helps to teach your dog self-control.

9. GET MAD! ARE YOU MAD?

This is a great trick for dogs/puppies who kick after
they have gone to the bathroom. The kicking, an

instinctive reaction to spread the smell of their urine/feces for other animals to smell, can be turned to a trick. Each time he kicks, say in an animated tone, "Are you mad? Get mad!" and quickly reward him. Over the course of time, he will learn the phrase and, when asked in the house, "Are you mad?" will be able to kick on command!

10. ROLL OVER

Another kid favorite. As soon as your dog lies down on the "down" command, use a treat to roll the puppy over. At first, you might need to physically (and gently) roll him over. As soon as he rolls completely over, get excited And say, "Good boy! Good rollover!" Repeat the command and process over and over. Each time make sure he rolls over—whether he does it himself or you physically roll him—so he understands that he must roll over to get the treat or verbal praise.

IV
Dogs in the Spotlight

Most Famous Dogs of Our Time

While today's Hollywood producers and directors have figured out the mass appeal of canine stars and are using them in anything from a sitcom comedy situation to an ad pitching mayonnaise or cars, dogs weren't always appreciated in Hollywood. They were often thought of as too time-consuming to be worth the effort. But a retired war dog, a feisty wirehaired fox terrier, and a dog named Lassie changed all that. As these canines' popularity soared, movie executives scrambled to find more dogs. Although the contributions of dogs in Hollywood are overwhelming, here are ten superstars who set the stage for animal actors as we know them today.

1. RIN TIN TIN

In September of 1918, as World War I was coming to a close, Corporal Lee Duncan discovered an abandoned German war dog station. Inside was a female German shepherd, protecting her litter of puppies. Knowing that she and her babies would starve, Duncan rescued the brood, adopting two of the pups for himself.

Nanette and Rin Tin Tin—named after the dolls French soldiers wore around their necks for luck—returned to the United States with Duncan, where he and Rin Tin Tin embarked on a movie career. Rin Tin Tin wowed audiences with his ability to fight, swim, leap, and play dead.

By the end of his career, he had appeared in twenty-four films, earned $1,000 a week, was insured for $100,000, and had his own production unit, limousine and chauffeur, orchestra for mood music, a diamond-studded collar, and chateaubriand steak prepared with all the trimmings by his personal chef. Rin Tin Tin died at the age of fourteen.

Today, Rin Tin Tin lives on. In 1957, the Hereford family acquired the bloodlines from Lee Duncan and has continued to raise, train, and love Rin Tin Tins V–IX. Rin Tin Tin VIII still makes appearances, but Rin Tin Tin IX will take over in 2004. (For more information about Rin Tin Tin and the Hereford Family, check www.RinTinTin.com.)

2. ASTA

The quirky character of Asta, the wirehaired terrier, became famous during 1930s and 1940s' *The Thin Man* movie series, starring William Powell and Myrna Loy. Everywhere the sleuthing couple, Nick and Nora Charles, went so, too, did Asta. In one scene, the couple is asked, with a dog like Asta, why would they want children? However, offscreen, things were not always so cozy. Because Asta's trainer felt that too much contact with the actors would ruin the dog's training, Asta had limited contact with Powell and Loy. In fact, Asta bit Myrna Loy during one particular scene. Despite this, Asta went on to star with other big names such as Cary Grant and Katherine Hepburn (in *Bringing Up Baby*).

3. **LASSIE**

When Lassie's (aka Pal's) owners were unable to stop him from chasing motorcycles and running away, he was given to a trainer, who made Pal/Lassie the star we know today. Lassie made his big debut in the 1943 movie, *Lassie Come Home*, starring Roddy McDowall and Elizabeth Taylor. Many have followed in the footsteps of the original Lassie, but Pal was the first. More than six decades later, the Lassie juggernaut is running strong with cartoons, a television show, and movies. Although no collie can compete with Lassie, it is important to note that a collie by the name of Blair is the first dog ever to star in his own movie, *Rescued by Rover*, filmed in 1904 and starring Cecil Hepworth.

4. **PETEY**

The original Petey appeared in 1922 when *Our Gang* (Little Rascals) first appeared, but there were a number of Peteys who appeared between the years 1922–44. Petey, the white pit bull with the magic marker circle around one eye, became one of the most recognizable and beloved dogs of the 1920s and 1930s—which explains why controversy continues regarding his final burial spot. Aspen Hill Pet Cemetery in Silver Spring, Maryland, is the burial place of a dog named Jiggs—said to be Petey. Many believe that while Jiggs was a "Petey," he wasn't *the* Petey, who is actually believed to be buried in the famous Pet Memorial Cemetery in Calabasas, California.

5. **MURRAY**

Before there was Moose, there was Murray, billed as one of the lead characters in the seven-year sitcom, *Mad About You*, starring Paul Reiser and Helen Hunt. In the show's September 1992 premiere, it was clear that Murray (aka Maui) was no ordinary dog. Throughout the series, Murray had a number of dog walkers, a few romances, and a penchant for chasing an imaginary mouse around the house that brought his character legendary status. The seven-year-old collie/shepherd mix was actually the second Murray. Maui replaced Smiley after one season when it was clear that Smiley was a little too active for the set. Initially, the idea was to have a dog be seen but not heard while the scenes were run. But Murray was too big, eventually taking over scenes just by walking into the bathroom and drinking out of the toilet as the couple talked about day-to-day life. Murray is one of the first dogs to prove the staying power of a lead dog in a successful television series.

6. MOOSE

Moose, a Jack Russell terrier, has reached a level of stardom few canines can match. As an actor on the longest-running sitcom, *Frasier*, Moose plays the adorable "Eddie"—a character so deeply rooted in the weekly plots that his bio is listed along with those of his human counterparts. And like so many successful TV comedy actors, Moose has starred in his own movie (*My Dog Skip* with Kevin Bacon and Diane Ladd); coauthored his autobiography with Brian Hargrove, *My Life As a Dog*; and appeared in his own calendar. This pin-up pup has also graced the covers of *Life*, *Entertainment Weekly*, and *TV Guide*.

7. TOTO MEETS BENJI

In 1934, trainer Carl Spitz introduced the world to a little cairn terrier named Terry, who starred in the movie, *Bright Eyes*, with Shirley Temple and in the Spencer Tracy movie, *Fury*, in 1936. But it was not until 1939 that Terry reached true stardom—in the role of Toto in the *Wizard of Oz* with Judy Garland. With fourteen movies under his belt and his own biography, *I, Toto*, little Terry proved that little dogs could act, too. Action/adventure dogs had primarily been larger breeds. (Carl Spitz also trained "Buck," a Saint Bernard actor in *Call of the Wild*, with Clark Gable). Forever known as Toto, the cairn changed the perception of little dogs, laying the groundwork for the next canine sensation in a small package—Benji. In 1973, a little floppy-eared mutt starred in the self-titled movie that was not only a big hit but evoked a huge interest in shelter dogs. Since the premiere, there have been four Benjis, the last one starring in the most recent movie, *Benji Returns: From Rags to Riches*, with a female terrier mix.

8. GIDGET

The late 1980s and early 1990s were a good time to be a dog actor in commercials. Selling anything and everything from cars and stereos to carpets and vacuum cleaners, a dog had the last say. When bull terrier Spuds MacKenzie came out swinging as the party animal for Budweiser, he (who was really a she) was everywhere. Spuds wore sunglasses, relaxed on the beach, partied with bikini-clad girls, and zoomed around in cars. Spuds was the ticket. Then came the 1994 "Run for the border" campaign, with the Taco Bell dog. Again, seen as a party-loving dog, this eight-pound, eleven-inch-tall Chihuahua was really "Gidget." A $200 million baby for Taco Bell, Gidget was arguably the biggest commercial sensation in canine history. Discovered walking down the boardwalk in California, the three-year-old dog was "looking large and in charge." Thus, history was made.

9. *AIR BUD*

This beautiful golden retriever, dubbed the Lassie of our times, was originally one of David Letterman's Stupid Pet Trick contestants, wowing the crowd with his ability to make baskets. But Buddy reached stardom with his 1997 movie, *Air Bud*. While it did take him ten minutes to put on his shoes (a requirement for the script done with the help of trainer Debra J. Coe), Buddy was able to sink two fifteen-foot free throws with only six attempts. In 1998, Buddy was honored at the Academy Awards as one of the "Greatest Animal Actors of all time," and was given an honorary Oscar for his performances. Since *Air Bud*, Buddy has gone on to star in a series of sports-related movies, showing his ability to play soccer and football as well.

10. **CINDY LOU**

Although Cindy Lou did not become famous on the big screen, she made it on Broadway, starring as "Sandy," the faithful sidekick in *Annie*. But what is so amazing about this dog is her humble background. When dog trainer William Berloni found the shelter dog, she was just days away from being put to sleep. She was incredibly antisocial, fearful of humans, and in poor health. Upon her capture, shelter workers found a collar that had been embedded in her neck—evidence that she had once been owned but presumably had run wild since she was about six months old. This amazing dog (with the help of her equally amazing trainer/owner) went from being a risk factor with humans to a star on Broadway in one of the most beloved productions of all time—dancing and prancing on stage with children.

Bonus Celebrity

While she hasn't signed a movie contract yet, Lucy became an instant hit on daytime TV. When her owner, comedian/talk show host Ellen DeGeneres, launched the Ellen DeGeneres Show in September 2003, thousands logged on in a contest to name the pup. The winning name was "Lucy," with more than eighteen thousand votes. Lucy made several appearances on the show with her own "walker" on staff. Being the boss's daughter does have its perks.

How to Break Your Dog into Showbiz

Approximately 80 percent of the top canine stars in movies, television shows, and commercials are rescue dogs. As one Hollywood animal agent said, shelter dogs have great character and unusually outgoing personalities. Once adopted, the dogs live and train with their trainers, where they get more one-on-one attention, affection, and training than the average pet. But there are certain criteria needed to make a dog a star.

1. GETTING ALONG WITH STRANGERS

Whether a future star hopes to find fame in television, movies, print work (modeling), or on the stage, the canine must be at ease being handled by multiple persons. Camera and sound crews, photographers, makeup artists, other actors/models, producers, and assistants are everywhere, including (sometimes) underfoot. Success mandates confidence around strangers.

2. GETTING ALONG WITH OTHER ANIMALS

All too often dogs are perfect around humans but fall apart around other dogs. Whether they want to play or fight, it becomes a huge production problem. Dogs on camera must be able to resist the urge to pounce on other animals and listen to and watch their trainer for cues.

3. BLOCKING OUT THE NOISE

As it is with other animals, the general chaos and hub-bub of the production set can be very distracting to and distressing for the everyday dog. People yelling, cameras clanking, horns sounding off, lights flashing, and radios blaring are all things the dog must be able to block out.

4. SITTING ON COMMAND

"Oh, that's easy," many will say. Yes, but can your dog sit on command with all of the distractions? Some of the most basic obedience commands can be the most taxing for an excitable or distracted dog. The "sit" must be rock solid.

5. SITTING AND STAYING ON COMMAND

A dog might be able to sit on command, but what about holding a stay for a prolonged period? In basic obedience, the single most important command is the sit. A dog should be able to hold a two-, three-, four-minute sit while cats walk by, other dogs howl, doors slam, and sirens roar. It is this kind of confidence and stability in a dog that makes a star.

6. **DOWN ON COMMAND**

7. **DOWN AND STAYING ON COMMAND**

8. **HOLDING A POSITION OR POSE**

Just as with the sit/stay and down/stay commands, a dog must be able to hold a position or pose for a particular shot. In dog shows, dogs must be able to hold perfectly still while judges run their hands over the dogs, analyzing their every aspect and angle. This is no different. While cameras are adjusted and lighting is set and reset, your dog must be able to hold his position. It is tiring and exhausting work.

9. **SHARING THE GLORY**

Dogs in the pictures make everything look so easy: it's easy to imagine your dog doing that very same thing and being paid for it! What you don't know is that it is common for several look-alike dogs (animals) to be used for one picture. What appears to be the work of one dog actually may be the work of several.

10. **FINDING AN AGENT**

No matter how wonderful or perfectly trained your dog is, you won't get the kind of work needed to be noticed without the proper representation. Talk to an animal-casting agent to learn how much time, money, and energy are involved in making a star.[1]

Casting Agencies for Animals

1. **HOLLYWOOD PAWS**

   www.hollywoodpaws.com

2. **ANIMALS ACTORS**

   www.animal-actors.com
   800-803-9606

3. **ANIMAL ACTORS AGENCY**

   www.animalactorsagency.com
   4103 Holly Knoll Drive
   Los Angeles, California 90027

4. **EXTRAS FOR MOVIES**

   www.extrasformovies.com

5. **HOLLYWOOD ANIMALS**

   www.hollywoodanimals.com

6. **CASTING 4 HOLLYWOOD**

   www.casting4hollywood.com

7. **ANIMAL ACTORS**

   www.animalactors.com
   E-mail: animalactors@groups.msn.com

8. **WAG 'N TRAIN, INC.**

   www.wagntrain.ca
   519-742-4000
   Toronto, Canada

9. **CRITTERS OF THE CINEMA**

   www.crittersofthecinema.com
   661-724-1929

10. **TRAINING UNLIMITED**

    www.miriamfields.com*
    540-659-8858
    Stafford, Virginia

*Miriam Fields created Comfort Trainer™, one of the best, most effective training tools on the market.

Top-Grossing Dog Movies of All Time

In the early 1920s, when Warner Brothers Studios was facing bankruptcy, a mild-mannered German shepherd named Rin Tin Tin turned the studio around and changed Hollywood's opinion of casting canine stars. *The Adventures of Rex & Rinty* (1935) proved to be a big moneymaker. Each of the following is a top-grossing movie that called for a leading canine to carry it.

1. *Good Boy!* (Liam Aiken, Molly Shannon, Mathew Broderick, 2003, MGM)
2. *All Dogs Go to Heaven* (animated, 1989, MGM)
3. *Beethoven* (Charles Grodin, Dean Jones, 1992, MCA)
4. *Benji* (1973, Vestron and others)
5. *The Incredible Journey* (1963, Disney)
6. *Lady and the Tramp* (animated, 1955, Disney)
7. *Lassie Come Home* (Roddy McDowell, Elizabeth Taylor, 1943, MGM)
8. *Old Yeller* (Dorothy McGuire, Fess Parker, 1957, Disney)

9. *101 Dalmatians* (animated, 1961, Disney)
10. *Air Bud* (Michael Jeter, Kevin Zegers, 1997, Buena Vista)

HONORABLE MENTION

Balto (animated, 1998, Disney)
Balto is part dog, part wolf.

Best Supporting Canine Actors

1. *Cujo* (Dee Wallace-Stone, Daniel Hugh Kelly, 1983, Republic Studios)
2. *The Fox and the Hound* (Mickey Rooney, Kurt Russell, 1981, Walt Disney)
3. *Milo and Otis* (1989, Columbia/Tri Star)
4. *My Dog Skip* (Frankie Muniz, Diane Lane, 2000, Warner Brothers)
5. *The Thin Man* (William Powell, Myrna Loy, 1934, Warner Brothers)
6. *The Wizard of Oz* (Judy Garland, 1939, Warner Bros.)
7. *Turner and Hooch* (Tom Hanks, 1989, Touchstone Pictures)
8. *Cats & Dogs* (Tobey Maguire, Alec Baldwin, 2001, Warner Brothers)
9. *Iron Will* (Mackenzie Astin, 1994, Walt Disney Pictures)
10. *The Shaggy Dog* (Fred MacMurray, Jean Hagen, 1959, Disney)

HONORABLE MENTION

Best in Show (Christopher Guest, 2000, Castle Rock Entertainment)

First Dogs in the White House

1. ABRAHAM LINCOLN AND FIDO (1861–1865)

While Fido never lived in the White House, it is interesting how closely the life of this mixed breed followed the life of his master. Reportedly, Lincoln and Fido were very close—it was not at all uncommon to see Fido following Lincoln around town—but when the Lincolns moved to Washington, D.C., it was decided that life in the big city would not be good for Fido. So Fido was left behind with friends of the family with the understanding that they never punish him for having muddy paws or tie him up in the backyard. He led a good life until 1865, when Lincoln was assassinated. Fido attended his master's funeral and in just one year he, too, would be assassinated by a drunken man in Springfield, Illinois. He was stabbed to death for playfully greeting a man who was sitting on a curb.[1]

2. WARREN HARDING AND LADDIE BOY (1921–1923)

Laddie Boy, an Airedale terrier, was one of the first First Dogs to show the power of the canine in the

White House. While his owner, President Warren G. Harding, was having difficulties with both administrative affairs and public relations, Laddie Boy proved to be more popular than his master and received more accolades for his diplomacy. Long before President George H. W. Bush's dog, Millie, would pen a best-selling book, Laddie Boy gave the first canine interview to the *Washington Star*. Today, there is a statue of Laddie Boy made of pennies that were collected by the Newsboys Association and melted down to make the copper statue. It stands in the Smithsonian Institution, reminding us of one of the most famous First Dogs.[2]

3. FRANKLIN D. ROOSEVELT AND FALA (1933–1945)

Fala, the Scottish terrier, went to live in the White House in 1940 and enjoyed an exciting life on the go. He traveled to Newfoundland to attend the Atlantic Charter Conference (with the President and Prime Minister Winston Churchill) and on to Mexico to inspect defense plants (again with the President and Mexican President Camacho). In 1943 and 1944, Fala traveled to Canada to attend the Quebec Conference, but it was his big trip to the Aleutian Islands that sparked the most controversy when he was reportedly (and accidentally) left behind. Republicans accused Roosevelt of spending millions of taxpayers' dollars to send a destroyer back to retrieve Fala. It was then that Roosevelt delivered his famous Fala speech. Addressing a Teamsters Union, the President defended Fala, saying he had expected personal criticism but Fala had not, and "his Scotch soul was furious."

Fala became so popular, a personal secretary was appointed to him to answer the thousands and thousands of letters from fans. In 1942, a movie was made about Fala and his life at Hyde Park, New York (his home away from the White House). Although he spent the rest of his days running and playing in Hyde Park, family friends said he never fully adjusted to life after the death of his greatest companion, FDR, in 1945.[3]

4. LYNDON B. JOHNSON AND HIM AND HER AND YUKI (1963-1969)

Him and Her, the most recognizable First Dogs of Johnson's presidency, were registered beagles. Many people still remember the 1964 photograph of the president lifting Him by his ears, which caused a huge protest among animal lovers.

Despite that picture, however, Johnson was known to be a great lover of dogs. After Her died (1964) at the White House, from swallowing a stone, and Him died (1967) when struck by a car while he was chasing a squirrel on the White House lawn and ran out into the street, Johnson received another beagle from J. Edgar Hoover. The pup, named J. Edgar but called, "J," moved to the LBJ Ranch when the Johnsons left the White House. But it was Yuki, a mixed breed rescued by Johnson's daughter, Luci, who caused the greatest sensation at the White House.

Initially, Yuki, named "Yukimas," which means "snow" in Japanese, only came to Washington, D.C. for a visit. But Yuki won Johnson over and soon became a great companion to the president. On Johnson's birthday, August 27, 1967, Luci presented Yuki as a gift to her father. Yuki and the president were often seen (and heard) singing together. Yuki was known to climb onto the president's lap in front of dignitaries from around the world, and both she and President Johnson would tilt back their heads to howl.[4]

5. RICHARD NIXON AND CHECKERS (1969–1974)

In 1952, while running for vice president on the Eisenhower/Nixon ticket, Nixon was confronted with a news story charging that he had a secret personal fund worth $18,000 under an assumed name. Rather than resigning from the campaign, Nixon chose to appeal to the American people on television. He remembered how FDR had defended his dog, Fala, in 1944 and decided to try the same defense. He explained that the gift was from a Republican in Texas, "a little cocker spaniel dog . . . black and white spotted. And our little girl, Tricia, the six-year-old, named it Checkers. And you know, the kids (like all kids) love the dog, and I just want to say this right now, that regardless of what they say about it, we're gonna keep it." His defense was based entirely on his love for his dog.

After the speech, Nixon cried, believing all was lost. But the speech, like FDR's, was a hit and Nixon remained on the ticket. Later, he would write, "Checkers emerged from the campaign the best-known dog in the nation since Fala."[5]

6. GERALD FORD AND LIBERTY (1974–1977)

President Ford loved his Liberty, a golden retriever given to him by his daughter, Susan, and his personal photographer, David Hume Kennerly. As the story goes, Kennerly did a little research and found a breeder to his liking in Minneapolis. He contacted the breeder and requested a puppy "for a friend." But the breeder wanted to know more about the would-be adoptive parents of this golden retriever. Kennerly reportedly said, "The couple is friendly. They're middle-aged, and they live in a white house with a big yard and fence around it. It's a lovely place." When asked if this couple rented or owned the white house, Kennerly replied, "I guess you might call it public housing."

While she lived in the White House, Liberty went through obedience training, learning a few extra tricks as well. Former White House staffers remember that if visitors stayed too long, Ford would whistle for Liberty to "pounce on them."

In her memoir, *The Times of My Life*, Betty Ford described the life and times of Liberty in the White House. On one occasion, while pregnant with nine puppies, Liberty desperately needed to go outside. President Ford put on his robe and slippers and took Liberty outside to the south lawn (at 3 a.m.) only to discover that he was locked out and couldn't get back in. He found an open stairwell, and the two climbed to the second and third floors only to find every door locked. Eventually, Secret Service agents found Ford and Liberty wandering the stairwell halls, trying to go back to bed.[6]

6. RONALD REAGAN AND LUCKY AND REX (1981–1989)

This author was on hand when a call came in to the Olde Towne School for Dogs in Alexandria, Virginia, from the White House. The Reagans were looking for a trainer for Lucky, their new Bouvier des Flandres. The prospect of training Nancy Reagan to handle (and train) an enthusiastic, powerfully built, eighty-pound puppy was daunting. Fortunately, the task was given to another trainer, and no one was surprised when Lucky retired to live on the Reagan's California ranch. While Lucky proved to be a great dog, too many times he nearly pulled Mrs. Reagan to the ground.

To replace Lucky, President Reagan bought his wife a new puppy—one-year-old and already trained Rex. The dog, a Cavalier King Charles spaniel, was named after Rex Scouten, the White House Chief Usher, who retired that same year (1985). Rex had belonged to William F. Buckley, who also owned Rex's brother, Fred. Rex proved to be a much better companion to the Reagans, but still pulled on his lead. During the Iran-Contra affair, as the Reagans were often dragged away from probing reporters, many wondered if that wasn't special trick of the eighteen-pound Rex.[7]

7. GEORGE BUSH AND MILLIE (1989–1993)

Millie came to live with George and Barbara Bush in February 1987, when Bush was vice president. She was given to the Bushes by a family friend after the death of their cocker spaniel. Like great First Dogs of the past, Millie was a common sight on the White House lawn and gained an instant following. To everyone's surprise, she was featured in *Washingtonian Magazine* as part of its Best and Worst series. Millie was dubbed "an Ugly Mutt" but became a cover girl for *LIFE* magazine in 1989, along with Barbara Bush and Millie's six puppies.

In 1990, Millie became the first White House dog to write a book. Dedicated to Barbara Bush, *Millie's Book* soon made the *New York Times* best-seller list—a particularly painful fact for many authors with just two legs and opposable thumbs.[8]

9. WILLIAM CLINTON AND BUDDY (1993–2001)

Buddy, the chocolate Labrador, became the unspoken leader of the dogs vs. cats war when he displaced the once-reigning Socks, the cat, and became a regular on the evening news, shown fetching toys for the President.

When Buddy arrived at the White House, there was some debate about what he would be named. The

Clintons tried Teddy and Luke, but Buddy, unim-
pressed, would not listen. Finally, everyone—including
their four-legged friend—was pleased with the name,
Buddy. Everyone, that is, except a man named Badi in
Jordan.

Coincidentally, the pronunciation of "Buddy" is the
same as "Badi" in Arabic, and, as dogs are still viewed
as scavengers in many countries like Jordan, the man
named Badi claimed to have been the subject of great
harassment. After Clinton named his dog Buddy, the
man stated, people in his country laughed at him and
implied he was like Clinton's dog.

While Clinton was dealing with the Paula Jones
lawsuits, Badi, the sheep trader from Jordan, sued
Clinton (unsuccessfully) for more than $4 million.

Buddy died at his home in New York in 2000 when
he was struck by a delivery truck.[9]

10. GEORGE W. BUSH AND SPOT AND BARNEY (2001–)

George W. isn't the only second-generation resident of
the White House. Spot, the only son of First Dog Millie,
was adopted by George W. and Laura Bush, becoming
the only second-generation First Dog. While Barney, a
Scotttish terrier, tends to keep a low profile, Spot
is well known for his energy and enthusiasm. The
entire Bush clan is known for its love of dogs. Although
the rule is "No Dogs Allowed" at the famous
Kennebunkport, Maine, summer home, the senior
George Bush has such a fondness for dogs that it's
impossible for him to turn them away, so the Bush
dogs do visit the compound.[10]

The Lassies

Lassie began as a short story, "Lassie Come Home," that appeared in the *Saturday Evening Post* in 1938. Author Eric Knight had no way of knowing that he was creating what would become an American icon. Just as Mom, apple pie, and hot dogs personified what was good and right about American life, so, too, did Lassie. Lassie brought hope, honesty, and love into our lives. For kids who grew up watching Lassie on Saturday afternoons, we knew the drill. She would get involved in some dangerous situation, trying to save her loved ones. She never complained, never gave up, and never disappointed us. Today, Lassie is stronger than ever. Here are some facts you may not know about her.

1. SHE WAS A HE

First of all, Lassie was a male. All the Lassies have been male dogs, even though the character is female. Male dogs are used for two reasons: Male collies do not shed their coats as females do, which helps production move more smoothly, and male collies are larger. This second reason is important because it allows the collie to play opposite a child actor for a longer period of time without the audience realizing the child is growing up.

In the original story, Lassie was also depicted as a tricolored collie, not the sable we have all come to know.

2. LIKE FATHER, LIKE SON

The tradition of Lassie has been passed down from father to son in both canine and human worlds. The current Lassie is the ninth-generation, direct descendent of the original Lassie. His trainer, Robert (Bob) Weatherwax is the son of the original trainer, Rudd Weatherwax. How close are these dogs and their trainers? The first Lassie was born on June 4, 1940, and Bob Weatherwax was born exactly one year later, on June 4, 1941.

3. THE REAL DEAL

The dog at Universal Studios Animal Actors show is not really Lassie, or any relation to Lassie. Universal leases the rights to use the name in its show, which features animal celebrity look-alikes. Lassie always appears with Bob Weatherwax. The folks at Colliewoode Productions assure you, if you don't see Bob Weatherwax, you didn't see the real Lassie.

4. A STAR WAS BORN

Lassie, aka Pal, was originally hired as a stunt dog. When the star collie refused to go into a raging river for a scene, Lassie was called in. The dog's performance— crossing the river, coming out exhausted, collapsing, near death yet still crawling in desperation to get to her master—made director Fred Wilcox say, "Pal may have gone into the water, but it was Lassie who came out. This is my star." The rest, as they say, is history.

5. CERTIFICATE OF HONOR

The first Lassie was awarded a U.S. Coast Guard "Certificate of Honor" for his part in a real-life rescue off Catalina Island. While traveling on Rudd Weatherwax's boat and anchored for the night, Lassie woke Weatherwax from a deep sleep and wouldn't stop barking until his master went to investigate. A small boat was drifting helplessly without lights or power with three people on board. Weatherwax towed the boat back to port, and Lassie was honored for his fast action in a time of need.

6. PAWOGRAPH

Lassie has his own "pawograph." Fans have always wanted a pawograph photo of Lassie, so Rudd Weatherwax had a cast made of the first Lassie's paw so he wouldn't have to worry about Lassie's feet. The original pawograph is still used today by the current Lassie and Bob Weatherwax. Fan mail can be addressed just to Lassie, and the California postal system delivers it to Lassie's doorstep. For a more direct route, you can contact Lassie & Co. at LassieNet@aol.com.

7. IT'S THE ONLY WAY TO GO

When Lassie flies on an airplane, he flies first class!

8. WHAT'S IN A NAME

In his book, *Lassie, A Dog's Life*, biographer Ace Collins identifies the Lassies by other names. In fact, the puppies are identified by other names simply as a way of sorting out which pup is which. But once a collie is chosen as successor, he becomes "Lassie" both publicly and privately for the rest of his life. The dog must become used to the name, Lassie, because this is how children and adults know him and call to him.

9. TRADEMARK LASSIE

"Lassie" is an international trademark and requires the living dog to have the following genetic qualifications: a rough collie with a sable and white coat, four feet tall, full white collar, white blaze on the nose.

10. THE ACTOR

Having appeared in hundreds of televisions shows, commercials, movies, print ads, and public appearances, Lassie has done and seen it all. He has danced with the Rockettes at Radio City Music Hall (1987), eaten lunch at the U.S. Senate (1967), and even appeared on *This Is Your Life*, hosted by Bob Hope. In 1968, Lassie was given an environmental award by President Lyndon B. Johnson. But it is the image of Lassie that has had the most profound impact on American culture. Lassie represents family and love. (For more information about Lassie, contact www.lassie.net.)

The Most Talked-About Dalmatians from *101 Dalmatians*

In 1961, when Walt Disney created the amazing story of two dalmatians, their puppies, and the evil Cruella de Ville, it was an instant hit. Drama, suspense, mystery, love, and comedy drew us in as the dalmatians captured our hearts. Although there were 101 of the spotted dogs, here are the favorites.

1. **Fidget**
2. **Jewel**
3. **Lucky**
4. **Patch**
5. **Pepper**
6. **Perdita**
7. **Pongo**
8. **Rolly**
9. **Spot**
10. **Wizzer**

HONORABLE MENTIONS

Kipper, the heroic Airedale, and **Towser**, the old barn dog, put themselves in danger to reunite Pongo and Perdita with their puppies and save all the other pups from Cruella de Ville and her henchmen.

The Real Story about Dalmatians

1. **THE EGYPTIAN DOG**

As unlikely as it sounds, the dalmatian dates back to the pharaohs. As early as 200 BCE, drawings of dalmatian-like dogs appeared in tombs and on grave markers. It is believed that genetic mutation was the initial reason for a spotted coat, but selective breeding continued to keep this unusual black on white (or liver on white) coat.

2. **DALMATIAN NAMED**

Throughout history, paintings have show hunting dogs, similar to the dalmatian, escorting or accompanying coaches. Initially, they were known as coach dogs, but in Thomas Bewicks's 1771 *History of Quadrupeds*, the spotted dog was given its first name—dalmatian.

3. **DOGS OF DALMATIA**

This breed is believed to have come from a country called Dalmatia on the Adriatic coast and transported across the world by seamen. Dalmatians were instantly popular for their distinguished appearance, but also because they made fine companions and guard dogs. To own one of these dogs was to be of significant standing in the royal courts.

4. COMING TO AMERICA

As in Europe, these dogs were an instant hit, although they were dogs of the working class in North America. Dalmatians were a favorite among the men on the horse-drawn fire wagons of the nineteenth and early twentieth centuries. As the wagon clambered down the street, rushing to put out a fire, the dalmatian's loud bark helped to clear the streets for the wagon team/firefighters. Today, they no longer help fight fires, but they remain a symbol for most firehouses: they are the "Firehouse Dog" mascot.

5. THE DALMATIAN GRIN

This breed is known for its lip-curling grin that often puts off non-dalmatian owners. When they are happily greeting someone or asking for play, the lip curls, exposing teeth. To the dalmatian lover, this is known as the spotted-dog salute: "Hi! Come play with me!" Interestingly, they do this only with humans.

6. THE TRUTH ABOUT *101 Dalmatians*

Just like the movie, this breed has been in great danger. Because people are often struck with the beauty of the dogs' coat, backyard breeding has been a problem. Just as with any breed, as the popularity of the dog rises, so, too, does the idea of making a profit. Little thought is given to proper bloodlines or characteristics. Check with a reputable breeder to make sure your dalmatian (or any purebred) is what he should be. Cruella de Ville, be gone.

7. SPOTTING

The dalmatian's two colors are black spots on a white coat or liver (brown) spots on a white coat. Liver and black are never together on a white coat. And just like snowflakes, every spotted dalmatian puppy is differ-ent—with different patterns and organizations of spots. Read more about proper spotting and how they are formed in a book about dalmatians or check the Dalmation Club of America, www.thedca.org.

8. DEAFNESS

Canine coats that are genetically white are often asso-ciated with hereditary deafness. Just as you should check with a reputable breeder for good bloodlines, you should also check the dog's hearing. Breeders can determine bilateral (both ears) or unilateral (one ear) deafness in their puppies.

9. THE CRAZY DALMATIAN

Dalmatians have a reputation of being nervous, nutty, or hyperactive. The truth is, this breed is no more hyperactive than Labrador retrievers or standard poo-dles. But like so many breeds, they need proper exer-cise and training. They are exceptionally intelligent dogs who need attention, stimulation, and praise. Like the Labrador, this coach dog can be destructive if not given an emotional and physical outlet.

10. NO ROLY-POLIES

Despite what the name, Roly, might tell you, dalma-tians are not chubby dogs by nature; they are lean, muscular, and powerful. When asked, most breeders and trainers of dalmatians will tell you that the most accurate portrayal of this breed from the *101 Dalmatians* book/movie is Pongo and Perdita—loyal and loving to the end. And, if you're having a really good time, what's another eighty-seven friends?[1]

Most-Loved Animated Dogs

Animated and cartoon dogs through have been plentiful, playing faithful sidekick, bumbling buffoon, bully, downtrodden, picked upon, avenging angel, prankster, and more. Since the turn of the twentieth century, dogs have played a huge part in American humor and literature. Even their cartoon characters illustrate how complex dogs are and what an integral part they play in our lives.

1. SANDY

When Little Orphan Annie first appeared in the *New York Daily* on August 5, 1924, Annie was a little orphan down on her luck but not her spirit. A shock of red, curly hair, a red dress, and a dog named Sandy were all she owned in this world. Sandy gave her comfort, companionship, and courage.

2. THE COMPLEX RELATIONSHIP OF GOOFY AND PLUTO

In 1927, along with a little-known mouse, Mickey, Pluto made his debut on the big screen. Happy-go-lucky Pluto followed Mickey around on his adventures, entertaining audiences around the world. So popular was he that Walt Disney created a new character—Goofy. Originally named Dippy Dawg, Goofy made his appearance in 1932 with two very distinct differences from his ancestor, Pluto: Goofy walked erect and could speak. With his signature pronunciation of "Garwsh," instead of "Gosh," Goofy lived as Mickey did, as a nine-to-five working, car-driving, clothing-wearing animal while Pluto stayed in the doghouse. This was the beginning of the evolution of the animated dog.

3. LADY AND THE TRAMP

Another duo that hit the big screen and made dog history was Lady and her unlikely friend, Tramp. Originally created in 1937, the story evolved around "Lady," who, when pushed out of the inner family circle by the arrival of a baby, embarks on a new adventure. But Walt Disney felt a new character with a new perspective on life needed to be added to the story. Tramp, previously known as "Happy Dan the Whistling Dog," offered insight from the other side of the tracks and, thus, Lady and the Tramp were born. In 1944, we learned how a cocker spaniel and a mutt lived, learned, and loved in a human world.

4. SNOOPY

Perhaps the world's most beloved character is the dog with the alter egos—the World War I Flying Ace, Joe Cool, the Vulture, friend to Woodstock the bird, and enemy of blanket-carrying boys—Snoopy. On October 2, 1950, the black and white beagle known as Snoopy was introduced to the world as Charlie Brown's dog. But by January 5, 1956, the dog who could and would not be walked on a leash; the Daisy Hill Puppy Farm dropout; the only dog known to man who, despite not having opposable thumbs, could type his memoirs atop his dog house, began walking on two legs. Snoopy led the way for dogs everywhere. He showed us that dogs do have fears, worries, and joy—and really big appetites.

5. MARMADUKE

Long before there was Scooby, there was Marmaduke—the Great Dane who helped himself to the entire couch, whatever was in the refrigerator, and all the milk the milkman had to offer. This comical super-sized dog was nationally syndicated, delighting readers for decades. Marmaduke was one of the first dogs who ruled the house from inside, and, despite the day-to-day irritations he caused his family, they loved him and would never part with him.

6. DINO THE PREHISTORIC DOG

In 1960, *The Flintstones* became television's first-ever, prime-time animated situation comedy. It was a huge success. The prehistoric bunch from Bedrock was the complete family, with Fred, Wilma, and their dinosaur/dog mix, Dino. This is a reminder that dogs have been with us since the cave days, and that a family isn't a family until it has a dog. As the longest-running cartoon, playing in more than seventy-three countries around the globe, there is no denying Dino's star power.

7. PONGO AND PERDITA

Most people identify this pair as simply two dogs from "101 Dalmatians," but any two dogs who could be biological/adoptive parents to 101 dalmatians need top billing. In 1960, Disney's movie, *101 Dalmatians*, appeared. The story revolves around the evil Cruella de Ville's attempts to kidnap Perdita's puppies in hopes of creating her very own dalmatian coats, but the complex relationship between these dogs takes center stage. It is the use of the "Dog Chain" that allows Pongo and Perdita to track down their fifteen stolen puppies and, with the help of many other dogs, are able save an additional eighty-six dalmatian pups from a horrible fate.

8. SCOOBY-ROOBY-DOO

Scooby Doo was originally had shaggy, long hair in an attempt to keep him from looking too much like Marmaduke. Throw in some "nosy, meddling kids," Scooby snacks, a mystery fan, and an insatiable appetite for crime and hot dogs and you've got Scooby and his gang—a band of crime-fighting teenagers and their dog. Debuting in fall 1969, Scooby became an international hit.

In 2002, an animated Scooby appeared in a remake with live-action actors Freddie Prinze, Jr., Sarah Michelle Gellar, and Matthew Lillard, and again in 2004 in *Scooby Doo 2: Monsters Unleashed*.

9. THE CAT'S DOG

On June 19, 1978, when the cartoon character of Jon Arbuckle adopted a cat named Garfield, a new sensation was born. The obnoxious, lasagna-eating, morning-hating cat ruled the house and made life miserable for Jon's dog, Odie. On the surface, Odie appeared to be nothing more than a drooling, mindless puppy looking for the next good game of catch. But Odie was true to the nature of the dog, always forgiving Garfield for his pranks, never begrudging another of his goodies or fun times, and, every once in a great while, taking particular delight in sticking it to the old feline.

10. A DOG NAMED BLUE

The greatest animated dog sensation in recent times appeared in 1996, when the television show, *Blue's Clues*, aired. Creator Angela Santomero was looking for something a little different and liked the idea of talking directly to the television audience. Using a real person inside an animated world, "Steve," and his animated puppy, Blue, spoke directly to the preschool-age audience with lessons in communication and critical thinking. Blue hides clues around her house for Steve and the audience to discover and reason out what game Blue wants to play. Once she puts a blue paw print on her clues, the game is on. Today, there are dozens of movies, books, toys, dolls, tapes, and more of a little dog named Blue.

HONORABLE MENTION

In the cartoon series, *For Better or For Worse*, by Lynn Johnston, the family dog was an old sheepdog named Farley. While Farley was not a main character in the series, he made cartoon history when he plunged into a river to save little April. No sooner did he make it to shore with the child than he collapsed, dying of a heart attack, reducing millions of readers to tears and reminding us all—even through cartoon fiction—how noble, selfless, and loving our four-legged friends are.

Most Popular Dog Fiction of All Time

1. ***CALL OF THE WILD***

In 1903, Jack London mesmerized the world with his tale of Buck, a sled dog in the Klondike, and his journey of transformation. Initially serialized in the *Saturday Evening Post* from June 20 through July 18, 1903, the story that captured so many hearts was turned into a book. Dozens of stories and movies are based on *Call of the Wild*.

2. ***WHITE FANG***

Just three years later, London followed up with a second successful dog story. In this tale of taming a wild dog, London skillfully comments on the treatment of animals by humans and the relationship between the two. *White Fang* was made into a movie, starring Ethan Hawke, in 1991.

3. ***LASSIE***

British writer Eric Knight created the story of the faithful collie, Lassie, living with her family in Yorkshire while they struggle through the depression. Like Jack London, Knight initially serialized the story in the *Saturday Evening Post* in 1938. The first book, *Lassie, Come Home*, was published in 1940. It was such a huge success in both the United States and Great Britain that the first movie about Lassie was made in 1943, followed by her television debut in 1954. While Lassie entertained us by rescuing people and animals from fires, raging rivers, mountain lions, and storms, the stories taught us about humanity and compassion.

4. *OLD YELLER*

In perhaps one of the biggest tearjerkers of all time, Fred Gipson created the story (1956) of a young boy and his dog living in a small town in central Texas in the 1860s. While the boy's father is away, fourteen-year-old Travis heads the household. After he adopts Old Yeller, the stray dog helps Travis to protect the family, but must be killed when he becomes rabid from fighting a rabid wolf. To this day, *Old Yeller* symbolizes the heartbreak of losing a loved one and growing up.

5. *THE INCREDIBLE JOURNEY*

In 1961, Canadian writer Sheila Burnford introduced the world to three loveable, lost pets—an old bull terrier named Bodger, a Siamese cat named Tao, and a youthful Labrador retriever named Luath—who must overcome dangerous obstacles to find their way home again. It is a story of courage, loyalty, and love that spurred the series of movies, *The Incredible Journey*, *Homeward Bound*, and *Homeward Bound II*.

6. *WHERE THE RED FERN GROWS*

The world was also introduced to two wonderful coonhounds in 1961. The dogs are adopted by a young boy, and the threesome romps through the Ozarks hunting raccoons. Old Dan and Little Annie display all the qualities of a good dog—companionship, trust, love, and total devotion. This story by Wilson Rawls remains one of the classics.

7. *CLIFFORD THE BIG RED DOG*

As a struggling illustrator, Norman Bridwell went from publishing house to publishing house until he got some sound advice—create a story to go along with the pictures. Among his pictures was an illustration of a large horse-sized bloodhound with a baby. Bridwell expanded on this, making the dog even bigger (and more red) to create Clifford the Big Red Dog. Emily, Clifford's owner, was based on the author's daughter. That was just the right combination—it has sold forty-four million copies worldwide and has been developed into a television series.

8. *GOOD DOG, CARL*

In 1985, a new hero was created in the dog world and, some would argue, just in time. While rumors swirled about the relationship between rottweilers and children, Carl showed us all how good rotties can be with kids. With adults seemingly unavailable, Carl feeds, baths, clothes, and cares for a baby. Author and illustrator Alexandra Day created a series from the best-selling books to entertain readers of all ages.

9. *MY DOG SKIP*

Before the loveable actor Moose (aka "Eddie" from Frazier) appeared on the big screen as "Skip," *My Dog Skip* was a best-selling book. In 1995, Willie Morris wrote his boyhood memoirs about growing up in the

1940s South with his favorite dog, Skip. It's the classic "Boy and His Dog" story.

10. *SHILOH*

Author Phyllis Reynolds Naylor tells the tale of a boy from rural West Virginia in need of a friend. When Marty Preston finds a young beagle, it's love at first sight, but it's also trouble as the beagle's owner is a mean-spirited, gun-totting drunkard who beats the dog. Marty tries to keep his friendship with Shiloh a secret from his family, but he is convinced the dog needs him. In fact, Marty needs Shiloh, too, and their mutual bond is the theme of this captivating story.

William Wegman and His Weimaraners

Weimaraners, Weimaraners, everywhere Weimaraners. Suddenly, they were everywhere—on calendars, posters, and greeting cards, in books, portraits, videos, and Polaroids. They read newspapers, wear clothing, and drive cars. Through art, these dogs reflected our culture. Who are these dogs, and how did they become so prominent in pop culture? Here are ten things you may not have known about Wegman's Weimaraners and the breed as a whole.

1. WILLIAM THE ARTIST

Wegman never envisioned working with dogs. In the early 1970s, Wegman was a solo artist without a clear vision of his talents, and, in fact, he didn't really want a dog; it was his wife's idea. Today, Wegman credits his dogs as full collaborators, saying it is the dogs that have great artistic intelligence and understand his work.

2. MAN RAY

Man Ray was the first Wegman Weimaraner model. He was a male Weimaraner pup who whimpered so much that Wegman began using the puppy in his photographs simply to keep him entertained and silent. Although Wegman claims the young pup was the instigator, Man Ray would go on to appear in dozens of publications, from books and calendars to posters and T-shirts, all over the world. The two worked together for twelve years.

3. FAY RAY

The beautiful, expressive Fay Ray is perhaps the best-known Wegman Weimaraner of the bunch. As Wegman's popularity began to rise, Fay Ray stepped into the spotlight, donning lavish outfits, posing for (among other things) the reimagining of Cinderella and Little Red Riding Hood. Fay Ray, thought to be Wegman's most loved pup, died just three weeks after having her last litter of puppies; she had been diagnosed with acute leukemia.

4. THE PUPS

Currently, the four Wegman Weimaraners are Crooky, Batty (aka Battina), Chundo, and Chips. Each has his or her own personality that brings even more life, humor, and drama to Wegman's work. Whereas Batty reportedly daydreams when she is being photographed, Chips is the consummate professional, always watching and waiting for direction.

5. THE FASHION DEMANDS

Those aren't just any old clothes we see on the Weimaraners. Wegman's dogs have been dressed by and posed in the clothing of some of the most famous (and expensive) designers in the world. Batty, Chundo, Crooky, and Chip have appeared in Jean-Paul

Gaultier, Helmut Lang, Alexander McQueen, Issey Miyake, Todd Oldham, and Ann Sui originals.

6. THE ORIGINS OF THE WEIMARANER

This breed is believed to be several centuries old. A Van Dyck painting from the early 1600s depicts the Weimaraner as a hunting/companion dog. The debate over its coloring continues today. Some contend that albinism came into the blood lines of early German pointing dogs, whereas others insist the Weimaraner is the descendent of the Braken. Most believe that this breed is the result of the Grand Duke Karl August of Weimar's crossbreeding a regular pointer and a yellow pointer.

7. MEET THE DOG

The Weimaraner is a bold dog. According to the American Kennel Club, this breed is smart—they have busy minds and thrive on activity. They are strong and determined and need time, space, and attention. If you relish the challenge of keeping ahead of the fearless "gray ghost," and your daily activities can include your dog, you may be suited to the Weimaraner. He loves kids, and he is used to being a member of the family. The Weimaraner is a member of the sporting group and was first recognized by the AKC in 1943.

8. TRAVELS OF THE WEGMAN WEIMARANERS

A retrospective of Wegman's work (and dogs) has traveled to museums throughout Europe and the United States, including to the Whitney Museum of American Art and the Children's Art Museum, both in New York City. His works can be seen in Japan and Sweden as well. Wegman's Weimaraners have also appeared on pop culture television shows *Saturday Night Live* and *Sesame Street*, and on PBS and Nickelodeon. The artist and his dogs received awards and grants from the National Endowment for the Arts in 1976, the New York Foundation for the Arts Honor in 1999, and the Guggenheim Fellowship in 1975 and again in 1986. All this honor was bestowed on a dog-loving visionary and his amazing canine family because, as Wegman himself says, his dogs have given something special and unexpected to the world of art.[1]

9. BEST IN SHOW

When the movie, *Best in Show*, parodying the behind-the-scenes activities at the Westminster Kennel Dog Show hit movie theaters, a star was born. "Beatrice," the neurotic show dog, quickly became a crowd favorite. According to Weimaraner breeder Heidi Warren of Northwoods Weimaraner Kennels, the portrayal of Beatrice was particularly amusing to Weimaraner owners. "This is an in-your-face breed who needs constant attention. Other dogs might be sitting by your side, Weims get in your lap." But the real joke is trying to tell who is more needy—the dogs or the owners. Warren notes that a majority of Weimaraner owners do not have children. These dogs are often treated like children. "They're children in little fun suits," says Warren.

10. THE REAL SHOW DOG—THE OTHER FAMOUS WEIMARANER

Her registered name is American Canadian Champion Norman's Greywind's Phoebe Snow, but her fans just called her Phoebe. Phoebe wowed Weimaraner lovers everywhere when she broke a thirty-two-year record, winning Best in Show at the Westminster Kennel Dog Show. During her career, she has won fourteen All Breed Best in Show and more than seventy-five Sporting Group titles. She held a Junior Hunting title and produced a Best in Show dog from one of her litters. She comes from a long line of champions: her father won Best of Breed at Westminster for three consecutive years, placed third in the Sporting Group, and was a multichampion in Best in Show.

After a string of championships, Phoebe left home at the age of two to live with professional handler Stan Flowers. Just as breeder Warren warned, the relationship between a Weimaraner owner and dog is intense. When Phoebe saw owner/handler Ellen J. Grevatt in the stands after a six-month separation, she had a typical Weimaraner reaction: "She screamed when she saw me," says Grevatt. "She didn't bark, she screamed, 'Mommy, mommy.' I cried, she cried. It was quite a reunion." Just like in the movies. (For more information about this breed, check out www.north-woodsweims.com.)

Canines in the Guinness Book of World Records

1. LONGEST DOG SWIM

On September 2, 1995, two black Labradors named Kai and Gypsy swam the "Maui Channel Swim" from Lanai to Maui in Hawaii. Alongside their owner, Steve Fisher, they made the 9.5-mile (15.2-kilometer) trek in six hours, three minutes, and forty-two seconds, a world record. The trio swam their way into the record books under the watchful eyes of an escort boat and the Maui Humane Society. What's next? Windsurfing and surfing.

2. HIGHEST JUMP BY A DOG

On September 27, 1993, an eighteen-month-old lurcher dog named Stag broke the canine high-jump record for a "leap-and-scramble" over a wooden wall without any climbing aids. Stag cleared a twelve-foot, 2.5-inch (3.72-meter) wall during a competition in Cirencester, Glos, United Kingdom, to earn the new record. Owners Mr. and Mrs. P. R. Matthews of Redruth, Cornwall, UK, entered their dog in the annual Cotswold County Fair.

3. FARTHEST TREK BY A CANINE

In 1923, a collie mix named Bobbie traveled an estimated 3,100 miles to reach his home in Oregon after
he and his owner were separated while on vacation in
Indiana. Crossing the Rocky Mountains alone, jockey-
ing through large cities and over dangerous rivers,
Bobbie returned to his home six months later.

4. SMALLEST DOG

The smallest dog on record was a Yorkshire terrier
from Blackburn, England. At the age of two—and fully
grown—this dog was just 2.5 inches tall (measured
from the shoulder) and 3.75 inches long from the tip
of his nose to the tip of his tail. Approximately the size
of a matchbox, he weighed just four ounces.

5. LARGEST DOG

In 1989, Zorba, an Old English mastiff, weighed in to
set a new world record. Measured from the tip of his
nose to the end of his tail Zorba was eight feet, three
inches, and he weighed 343 lbs.

6. HIGHEST-ALTITUDE SKYDIVE

On May 20, 1997, Brutus, a miniature dachshund,
jumped from a twin-engine plane with his owner, Ron
Sirull, to break a world record. The jump was 15,000
feet (4,572 meters) above sea level. Flying above
Lake Elsinore, California, Brutus (wearing his own
custom-made gear, including goggles) and his owner
have made more than seventy jumps.

7. LONGEST SCENT TRACKING

In 1925, a Doberman pinscher named Sauer tracked a
thief across South Africa for more than a hundred

miles (160 kilometers). Working with his partner, Detective Sergeant Herbert Kruger, and traveling over the arid Great Karroo plateau, Sauer refused to give up the chase and eventually captured the fugitive by scent alone.

8. SKIPPING ROPE

Picture this: In 1988, a long-legged Russian wolfhound named Olive Oyl, sporting ribbons in her hair, set the world record for most consecutive jumps with a jump rope, completing sixty-three rotations. Owners Alex and Paula Rothacker of Illinois taught Olive Oyl the word "up," using it each time she jumped. Before they knew it, they had a world-class jumper. (Olive Oyl was already a seasoned athlete, having once held the world record for the highest freestyle jump.)

9. OLDEST DOMESTIC DOG

An Australian cattle dog named Bluey lived to be twenty-nine years and five months old, working his farm and protecting his sheep against wild dogs until he was no longer able to tend his charges due to arthritis. Bluey was euthanized in 1939.

10. PUPPIES GALORE

The largest recorded litter of puppies born to one dog was brought into the world by a foxhound named Lena. Lena had twenty-three puppies on February, 11, 1945. This remarkable birth was not reported in *Guinness* until 1963.

Canine Cover Models
for *Sports Illustrated*

Say "cover model" and *Sports Illustrated* in the same sentence and visions of bikini-clad women come to mind. But long before there were women in bikinis on the cover, *Sports Illustrated* periodically featured dogs in that coveted space.

1. GREAT DANE

On February 14, 1955, the first dog appeared on the cover of *Sports Illustrated*. Volume 2, issue 7 of the magazine featured a Great Dane. The collaboration of writer Arthur Singer and photographer Ylla captured the true beauty of the great beast at just twenty-five cents a copy.

2. BULLDOG

In 1955, the bulldog celebrated Independence Day on the cover of *Sports Illustrated* in volume 3, issue 1. Top Dog Kippax Fearnought was captured by photographer Jerry Cooke/writer Reginald Wells for just twenty-five cents a copy. That's $7.50 for a year's subscription.

3. DACHSHUND

The beautiful Jewell and Adele graced the cover of the magazine on December 12, 1955, in volume 3, issue 24. The dachshunds were featured by photographer Richard Meek and writer Reginald Wells.

4. AFGHAN

Photographer Jerry Cooke returned with the majestic Taejon of Crown Crest—the champion Afghan hound. The Afghan appears on the cover of volume 4, issue 11, on March 12, 1956.

5. BULLDOG

The bulldog returns, this time as a college mascot. Handsome Dan IX of Yale appears on the November 5, 1956, issue, covering the Yale-Dartmouth Weekend. Photographer Jerry Cooke featured the famous mascot in volume 5, issue 19, on the football field, alongside a Yale megaphone.

6. BOXER

In volume 6, issue 6 of *Sports Illustrated*, Barrage of Quality Hill, the champion boxer appears on the cover. In this February 11, 1957 issue, photographer Jerry Cooke and writer Alice Higgins present the beautiful side of the powerful boxer.

7. PHEASANT SHOOT

This January 19, 1959 issue of *Sports Illustrated*, celebrates the spirit of the hunting dog as photographer Toni Frissell captures the intensity of the bird dog in a Nevada blizzard. "Pheasant Hunt" is volume 10, issue 3.

8. RETRIEVER CHAMPIONSHIPS

Continuing the celebration of hunting dogs, photographer Toni Frissell chose the Chesapeake Bay retriever to grace the cover of the November 30, 1959, volume 11, issue 22 of *Sports Illustrated*, with its coverage of the National Field Trials.

9. BEDLINGTON TERRIER

In volume 12, issue 6 of *Sports Illustrated*, writer John G. Zimmerman takes a hard inside look at dog shows, including the Westminster. In this February 8, 1960, issue, the Bedlington terrier serves as the cover model, with the lead title, "Are Dog Shows Ruining Dogs?"

10. OLD ENGLISH SHEEPDOG

Under the lead title, "Big Itch in the Dog World," the Old English sheepdog was chosen by photographer Lane Stewart to complement writer Robert H. Boyle's piece on dogs and dog shows. Champion Sir Lancelot of Barvan appeared in the February 24, 1975, volume 42, issue 8 copy.

Beware of Dog

In 1964, Sports Illustrated tried out a cover called Swimsuit Fashions and never looked back. Suddenly, coverage of the Westminster Dog Show was less appealing, and it would be another fifteen years before a dog would grace the cover of the prestigious magazine again. Since 1975, only one dog has been placed on the cover—an image of a ferocious-looking pit bull with the caption, "Beware of this dog."

Dogs in College
Top College Mascots

Throughout history, dogs and humans have been constant companions. They have fought battles, won wars, explored, herded and protected other animals, and created new lives together. Therefore, it seems only fitting that they should share college life as well. And, in fact, colleges and universities around the nation have chosen specific breeds of dogs, for one reason or another, to represent them. Hundreds of colleges have declared dogs as their symbol of strength, determination, and courage. Some of these institutions of higher education are fiercely proud of their mascots, others simply have no clue why they are represented by a greyhound or a retriever. The top ten list illustrates the proud, the unusual, and the amusing.

1. TEXAS A&M

Perhaps no university is more proud of its mascot than the Corp of Cadets at Texas A&M. The first live mascot was a stray mutt accidentally struck by a car filled with A&M cadets in 1931. The Aggies brought the dog back to their barracks and nursed her back to health.

The dog howled every time the bugler called reveille, so she was named Reveille. After her death in 1944, she was replaced by a collie and the tradition was in place.

Today, Reveille, the "First Lady of A&M," is also the highest-ranking cadet in the corps. Freshman must address her as "Miss Reveille, ma'am." She is assigned a sophomore to care for her during the year—a great honor among the cadets. In the dorm, the occupant of whichever bunk she chooses as her bed is forced to sleep on the floor. And, should Rev bark during class, professors are encouraged to dismiss the students. Reveille has spoken!

Reveille I and her successors are buried at the end of the tunnel leading into A&M football's Kyle Field. Legend has it that the dogs all face the football scoreboard so they'll always know the outcome of the game.

2. UNIVERSITY OF GEORGIA

In the 1920s, *Atlanta Constitution* writer Morgan Blake wrote, "The Georgia Bulldogs would sound good because there is a certain dignity about a bulldog, as well as a ferocity." During this time Georgia had strong ties with Yale, which also had the bulldog as its mascot, so the idea was well received. But the university did not officially adopt its first bulldog until the late 1940s, with a bull named Butch. In 1955, Uga stepped in to support his team, beginning the line of Ugas. Today, Uga VI cheers his school on, watching games from an air-conditioned doghouse near the cheerleader's platform.

The Ugas of the past are entombed in the walls of Sanford Stadium, near the main gate. A small bronze statue and a memorial plaque for each heroic football mascot is on display.

3. THE DOGS OF GEORGETOWN UNIVERSITY

While the Aggies do love the tradition of Reveille, what school could have a lengthier canine history than Georgetown University? In its early history, in the nineteenth century, the school ran a farm alongside the campus that employed several farm dogs, including a terrier named Rough and Ready and a bulldog named Pompey Gavin. The two didn't see eye to eye, and in 1862, Pompey Gavin killed Rough. The students held court and ruled that Pompey Gavin would be banished from campus.

There have been Labradors, a Russian wolfhound, bull terriers, and mixed breeds, but in the 1950s it was decided that the spirit of the bulldog best suited Georgetown University and was named their mascot.

4. JOHN JAY COLLEGE OF CRIMINAL JUSTICE–CITY UNIVERSITY OF NEW YORK

Until recently, the only evidence from a canine admissible in U.S. courtrooms has been from the bloodhound. Whether tracking convicted felons, suspected rapists, bank robbers, child molesters, or murderers, the work of these dogs is greatly respected in the courts. So, it is no great surprise that John Jay College of Criminal Justice would choose such a breed to represent the school. Capable of picking up a scent that is days old, the bloodhound is persistent, powerful, and determined.

5. SOUTHERN ILLINOIS UNIVERSITY

In 2002, colleges around the nation voted for their favorite Mascot of the Year. Only one dog mascot made the final twelve—the University of Tennessee's Smokey, a bluetick coonhound. The criteria for mascots were that they should be unique to their university or their area of the country. With coonhounds galore in Tennessee, and over fifty bulldog college mascots, what could be more original than the saluki of Southern Illinois Universitys' Little Egypt?

The first saluki made his appearance on the SIU campus during homecoming festivities in October 1951. One of the oldest known purebred dogs in the world, this ancient Egyptian breed was the perfect mascot for the university because of its geographical location—Little Egypt. Near the Carbondale campus is the convergence of both the Ohio and Mississippi rivers at Cairo, Illinois, which known as "Little Egypt." Now, it is the characteristics of the dog that appeal to the school—strong, fast, brave, and social.

6. UNIVERSITY OF WASHINGTON

Originally known as the Washington Vikings, the students and faculty decided after World War I that they wanted something more suitable to their own state, something that personified who they were. Both malamute and husky were popular suggestions, and an election was set for the student body, faculty, and fans to choose between them. At halftime on blustery February 3, 1922, football team captain Robert Ingram announced to the fans and student body that the husky was the official mascot of the university.

The breed, a native of Siberia, was brought to Alaska in 1909 but quickly became popular throughout Canada and the northern United States. Social, quick, agile, hearty, rambunctious, and powerful, the Washington Huskies was the perfect fit.

7. UNIVERSITY OF MARYLAND-BALTIMORE COUNTY

Shortly after the campus opened in fall 1966, a contest was conducted to choose a mascot for the school. On

October 19, 1966, the Chesapeake Bay retriever was chosen, and True Grit, a gift from champion breeder Claude Callegary, found his new home. A bronze statue of True Grit now stands in front of the UMBC's Retriever Activities Center, at the entrance to the campus. Students rub his nose before finals for luck, and he dons a cap and holds a diploma for graduation each year.

8. THE CITADEL

As a gift from the class of 2003, the Corps of Cadets received their first live bulldog mascot—paid for through private fund raisers and contributions. Although the bulldog has been the official mascot of The Citadel since 1908, the cadets undertook the new task of bulldog detail when, in 2003, the campus welcomed a ten-week-old, fifteen-pound English bulldog named General. Boo, the second mascot, a realtive of Uga the 5th of Georgia, was brought in to help relieve the social calendar of General. Because mascots are expected to appear at all events, including military events, Boo is a great help to General.

9. MORAVIAN COLLEGE

Tracing its founding to 1742, this college is recognized as the sixth-oldest college in the United States, following Harvard (1636), William and Mary (1693), St. John's in Annapolis (1696), Yale (1701), and the University of Pennsylvania (1740). With such noble roots, it is no surprise that the greyhound was chosen to represent this school, set in lovely Bethlehem, Pennsylvania. The history of the greyhound is also rich, dating back to the pharaohs. Greyhounds are known to be courageous, loyal, swift, and aristocratic—what other mascot could Moravian College have chosen?

The Citadel

The Citadel's bulldog mascot "General."

10. UNIVERSITY OF TENNESSEE

In 1953, the student body elected to have the native coonhound serve as its mascot. At halftime during a football game, dozens of coonhounds were brought out to be judged by the student body and fans. When the late Reverend Bill Brooks stepped forward with his prize-winning blue tick coonhound, "Brooks' Blue Smokey," the dog barked. When the crowd cheered, he threw his head back and barked again. This continued until Smokey had whipped everyone into a frenzy and a star was born!

In 1955, Smokey II was dognapped by Kentucky students and later had an altercation with the Baylor Bear mascot at the 1957 Sugar Bowl. In 1991, after Smokey VI suffered from heat exhaustion, he was placed on the Volunteers' injury list until his return to the mascot game later in the season. Smokey is one of the most loved figures in the state, so it is no wonder he made the list for "Mascot of the Year." He is famous for leading the Volunteers out of the giant "T" before each game. Smokey VIII, in his eighth season, is the winningest Smokey, with two Southeastern Conference titles and the 1998 national championship.

Mush! Top Sled Dog Races of All Time

Youngster Rachael Scdoris, with her lead dogs Johnny and Duchess from Bend, Oregon, became the youngest musher in history to finish a five hundred-mile sled dog race when she finished the International Pedigree Stage Stop sled dog race at the age of sixteen years and five days. Celebrated as a female athlete to watch[1], Scdoris made history again when she campaigned to compete in the Iditarod. Together with her father, athlete/trainer Jerry Scdoris, she compiled a list of the ten most notable sled dog competitions.

1. IDITAROD

This annual run is the most famous of all the races, making a 1,150-mile journey for competitors under the harshest conditions.

2. ALL-ALASKAN SWEEPSTAKES

This 408-mile run from Nome to Candle, Alaska (and back again) was established in the early 1900s.

3. OPEN NORTH AMERICAN CHAMPIONSHIPS

This annual sprint race in Fairbanks, Alaska tests the explosive power of the sled. The race was first run in the early 1950s.

4. FUR RENDEZVOUS

Also started in the early 1950s, this annual sprint race is held in Anchorage, Alaska.

5. LACONIA WORLD CHAMPIONSHIPS

Established in the 1920s, this sprint race is run in eastern North America in Laconia, New Hampshire.

5. PAS WORLD CHAMPIONSHIPS

Also established in the 1920s, this race is held in The Pas, Manitoba, Canada.

6. YELLOWKNIFE CANADIAN CHAMPIONSHIP

The Annual Dog Derby in Yellowknife, Northwest Territories, began in the 1950s, honoring the strongest teams in competition.

7. ASHTON AMERICAN DOG DERBY

This annual one hundred-mile race has been held in Ashton, Idaho, since the early 1920s.

8. YUKON QUEST INTERNATIONAL

Held in Whitehorse, Yukon Territory, Canada, every year, this one thousand-mile race is run to Fairbanks, Alaska, in the most extreme weather conditions.

9. and 10.   **ATTA BOY 300–THE OREGON WORLD CUP STAGE RACE AND INTERNATIONAL PEDIGREE STAGE STOP SLED DOG RACE (TIE)**

The first race, held in Bend, Oregon, is only two years old (first run in 2001) and lasts seven days. The second, an eight-day stage race held in Jackson Hole, Wyoming, has been in existence since 1996.

Top Mushers of All Time

1. **GEORGE ATTLA AND LEAD DOG LINGO**

Born in the 1930s, Attla was an Athabascan Indian from Huslia, Alaska. As a multiple World Sprint champion and top dog breeder, Attla (and Lingo) had a huge impact on the sledding world.

2. **SCOTTY ALLEN AND JOHN "IRON MAN" JOHNSON (TIE)**

Both dominated the early 1900s' sled dog races in Alaska.

3. **LEONARD SEPPALA AND LEAD DOG TOGO**

Both Seppala and Togo were part of the legendary run to Nome, Alaska in 1925 to retrieve the lifesaving diphtheria serum (on which the movie *Balto* was based). Seppala was a top-winning sled dog racer in the early 1900s. Today, a line of registered Siberian huskies carries the name Seppala.

4. JOE REDINGTON, SR.

Known as the "Father of the Iditarod," Redington is credited with founding the legendary run and is a modern day legend in the sport of dog sled racing.

5. GARETH WRIGHT AND LEAD DOG JENNY

This Athabascan Indian, born in the 1930s, reigned as world champion and influential dog breeder from Fairbanks, Alaska, where he still lives today.

6. RICK SWENSON AND LEAD DOG ANDY AND SUSAN BUTCHER AND LEAD DOG GRANITE (TIE)

Both are multiple Iditarod champions and both live outside Fairbanks, Alaska, today. Butcher became one of the most notable mushers in recent years and a favorite female athlete. Featured in *Sports Illustrated*, various fitness magazines, and women's sports books, Butcher remains a big name in the sled dog circuit.

7. LIBBY RIDDLES AND LEAD DOGS AXEL AND DUGAN AND JOE RUNYAN AND LEAD DOG FURLEIN HUSKY (TIE)

Riddles was the first woman to win the Iditarod in 1985, and Runyan is the only musher to have won the Yukon Quest, the Iditarod, and the Alpirod. Today, Riddles lives in Homer, Alaska, and Runyan lives in New Mexico.

8. TERRY STREEPER AND LEAD DOG HOP

With multiple world and Canadian championships under his belt (or sled), Streeper acts as a partner, coach, and manager for his brother, son, and daughter in the world of racing. He continues to be a force as a competitor, influential breeder, and trainer. Today, he lives with his family in Fort Nelson, British Columbia, Canada.

9. **ROXI WRIGHT AND LEAD DOGS PLUTO AND JOHNNY**

As the daughter of legendary musher Gareth Wright, Roxi has also made history as a world-class sprinter. She lives in Fairbanks, Alaska.

10. **DR. ROLAND LOMBARD AND LEAD DOG NELLIE**

A multiple world-class sprint champion, Roland heralded from the east coast—Wayland, Massachusetts. Roland is now deceased.

V
Canine Health

How Your Dog Can Improve Your Health

A beautiful Native American folktale depicts how the world was created: through the imagery of color and nature, the story describes the origin of all the animals . . . except, that is, for the dog. Why? Because Native Americans naturally assumed that when the first man walked the earth, viewing what wondrous animals had been brought forth, his dog would be right there with him to see the newest creations.

As history has told and retold it, the relationship between humans and dogs has endured through centuries of good times and bad. In fact, new studies show us that we humans are probably in much better health *because* of our dogs. Here's why.

1. THE FIT FACTOR

People who own dogs tend to be in better condition because they walk more than people who do not. Whether owners are apartment dwellers who have to walk to a specified dog area or responsible pet lovers who want to give their dog adequate exercise, dog owners are more active.

2. LONG-TERM MAINTENANCE

Because of the responsibility that pet owners feel, senior citizens who are dog owners are also (overall) in better condition than others their age. Walking and caring for another being requires owners to be more active, more outgoing, and more nurturing and, therefore, more in touch with their own needs than people without pets.

3. LOWER BLOOD PRESSURE

Pet owners over the age of forty have lower blood pressure and have 20 percent lower triglyceride levels than people their age without a pet.

4. AN APPLE A DAY

Or, better yet, a pet and a nuzzle a day keeps the doctor away. People who own indoor pets typically need to see doctors less often than nonpet-owning people. This is one of the reasons retirement and assisted living communities use the services of animal clubs or shelters to develop a bond between their residents and loving dogs. The love of a dog is all-powerful!

5. DEPRESSION AND/OR LONELINESS

The soft, knowing expression of a sweet dog needs no words. When we are feeling blue, our best friend is most often our dog. For this reason, senior citizen organizations use dogs, and children stricken with cancer and other life-threatening illnesses, abuse, and/or neglect are paired with therapy dogs. Caregivers who work with the elderly and the sick or needy report that contact with animals makes patients stronger, healthier, and happier, and research studies are beginning to support those observations.

6. LIFESAVER

According to the National Institute of Mental Health, the second leading cause of death among twenty-somethings, just after automobile accidents, is suicide. While suicide is a growing concern among physicians and mental health experts, we are seeing a countering trend—concern about animals. People who have considered suicide often report that, out of love and/or concern for their dogs (or cats), they were unable to go through with the act. Sometimes sudden changes or requests made by a dog owner—to care for a pet, for instance—have alerted family members that something is wrong. They frequently discover that their loved one was contemplating suicide. In his book, *For the Love of Your Dog*, former Olympic diver Greg Louganis discusses how his health status (HIV-positive) and a string of bad relationships led him to a suicide attempt. It was only because of his dogs, he says, that he did not carry out his deadly plan.

7. ALLERGIES

For nearly a century, many mothers haven't allowed dogs in the house because they were sure that pets were the cause of allergies. A recent study from the Allergy and Immunology Department at the Medical College of Georgia in Augusta supports the fact that children who grow up in a house with indoor pets have a lower risk of developing common allergies and asthma, defying everything we ever thought about our four-legged friends making us sniffle and sneeze.

8. THE LOSS OF A SPOUSE

The loss of a spouse is one of the most traumatic things that can happen in our lives. There is often rapid deterioration of the surviving spouse's health—particularly among senior citizens. Those with canine companions fare much better than nonowners do, because the dogs offer comfort, support, a daily routine to keep the mind distracted (or comforted), security, and love.

9. LAUGHTER

We are most at ease with our dogs. With no one else around, we tend to be more relaxed while we're talking and playing with Fido. While it may seem to be a small thing, experts agree that the small chuckles and giggles our dogs elicit from us while begging for a bag of potato chips or leaping wildly about for a squirrel are incredibly healthful—de-stressing us and lightening our mood.

10. SECURITY

Throughout the history of humans and dogs, the one constant demand we have made of our canine friends is to offer security. Even the smallest breeds have done just that, barking to alert us to strange noises, fighting animals both small and large, protecting our homes against invaders, and barking fiercely when a rogue squirrel is on the loose. We enter our homes with more ease, sleep better at night, and feel more comfortable in our homes because of our dogs.

Breeds that Are Most Susceptible to . . .

Dr. Earl Mindell's *Nutrition and Health for Dogs* gives a complete breakdown of some of the most dangerous and/or prevalent diseases dogs face today. Cancer, hip dysplasia, kidney failure, heart disease, liver disease, and seizures are major concerns for veterinarians and pet owners. Learn more about the breeds that are most susceptible and educate yourself about these illnesses/diseases.

Dogs Most Susceptible to Cancer

1. Boxer
2. Beagle
3. Collie
4. Dalmatian
5. German Shepherd
6. Retriever (Labrador, Golden)
7. Great Dane
8. Poodle (Toy, Miniature, Standard)
9. Pug
10. Weimaraner

Steps toward Cancer Prevention

1. SUN EXPOSURE

Yes, your dog can get a sunburn as well as skin cancer. Particularly for dogs with a white coat/pink skin or a thinner coat, sunburn can be a very serious problem. Be sure to apply sunscreen to your dog if he is vulnerable before heading outdoors, especially on a light-colored nose.

2. NO SMOKING

You've read all the studies and know that smoking around small children is very harmful to their health, potentially causing asthma and bronchitis as well as risking exposure to cancer. You're other baby—the four-legged one—is also at risk. If you have to smoke, do so outside, away from the family.

3. WE ARE WHAT WE EAT

Cheaper dog food is just that—cheap. Fillers (cereals) are the main component of those brands, robbing your dog of needed nutrients. By purchasing high-quality dog food, you are safeguarding against certain diseases. Veterinarians also suggest adding greens to your dog's diet. Add one-quarter cup of green beans or broccoli to his meal to help fight cancer.

4. PESTICIDES AND HERBICIDES

Again, we are what we eat. Be sure to wash all veggies your dog eats and keep him away from chemicals that might be sprayed on your lawn or those of your neighbors'. If you believe that your dog has walked through pesticides, be sure to wash his feet.

5. SPAY/NEUTER

You can fight ovarian or testicular cancers by having your dog spayed or neutered. In addition to combating pet overpopulation in this country, you will lengthen the life of your pet.

6. STAY FIT

Just as with humans, dogs that exercise regularly are least likely to have breast, uterine, or prostate cancer. To ensure a healthier, happier dog, begin an exercise program for the both of you.

7. GROOMING

If you groom your pet every day or every other day, constantly running your hands over him, you will be able to feel any unusual bumps or lumps. An ounce of prevention . . .

8. REGULAR CHECKUPS

Even the most dedicated groomer might miss something that only a vet will pick up. By keeping your dog up-to-date with his medical shots and evaluations, you and your vet can help prevent a disease or detect it while it is still curable.

9. DON'T DENY

If you feel a lump, call the vet for an appointment. Most likely, it's not going to go away by itself. And if something like cancer is caught soon enough, your vet may be able to stop it from spreading. It may also be nothing more than fat—a very common medical condition among older dogs. You won't know until you ask.

10. **WHEN THE NEWS IS BAD**

An oncologist can tell you more about the particular
kind of cancer your dog has, the breeds most susceptible to different kinds of cancer, and their survival
rates. Texas A&M, Ohio State, University of Pennsylvania, and Purdue have some of the most progressive veterinary schools studying cancer today.

Breeds Most Susceptible to Hip Dysplasia

Hip dysplasia is a degenerative condition in which the
head of the femur or thigh bone does not fit properly
into the acetabulum or hip socket. As the puppy
grows, the ball of the hip joint and the shallow cup of
the joint, or the "ball and socket," become malformed,
causing the dog great irritation and pain. Severe
arthritis can result from this disease and made worse
by excessive weight gain. Many owners are baffled by
the disease because its symptoms may appear to
come and go during the puppy's growing process. But
there is no missing the pain experienced as arthritis
sets in for the older dog. In more progressive cases, a
young dog may also experience instability, pain, and
arthritis. For more information about the disease, possible treatments, and signs to look for, log on to
www.vetinfo.com/ddyspla or www.cah.com/library/
hipdysp.html.

1. Airedale
2. American Cocker Spaniel
3. Great Dane
4. German Shepherd
5. Great Pyrenees
6. Husky
7. Newfoundland

8. Mastiff (Neopolitan, Tibetan)
9. Retriever (Labrador, Golden)
10. Setter (Irish, Gordon)

Breeds Most Susceptible to von Willebrand's Disease or Blood Clotting

Von Willebrand's Disease (vWD) is a common inherited canine bleeding disorder in which the blood clotting process is disrupted. Most dogs with vWD lead normal lives if the bleeding is treated appropriately. Common symptoms are nosebleeds, bleeding of the gums, or prolonged bleeding from the umbilical cord at birth or when the pup loses its baby teeth. Although any breed (mixed ones included) can have von Willibrand's disease, some are more prone to it than others. To learn more about the disease, treatments, and more breeds listed as vWD candidates, log on to www.vetinfo.com/dvonwillebrands.html.

1. Boxer
2. American Cocker Spaniel
3. Doberman Pinscher
4. German Shepherd
5. Retriever (Golden, Labrador)
6. Manchester Terrier
7. Miniature Schnauzer
8. Old English Sheepdog
9. Shetland Sheepdog
10. Scottish Terrier

Breeds Most Susceptible to Kidney Failure

1. Cocker Spaniel
2. Basenji
3. Beagle

4. Brittany
5. Chow Chow
6. Doberman Pinscher
7. German Shepherd
8. Lhaso Apso
9. Norwegian Elkhound
10. Standard Poodle

Breeds Most Susceptible to Heart Disease

1. American Cocker Spaniel
2. Beagle
3. Boxer
4. Cavalier King Charles Spaniel
5. Doberman Pinscher
6. Fox Terrier
7. German Shepherd
8. Great Dane
9. Irish Wolfhound
10. Samoyed

Breeds Most Susceptible to Liver Disease

1. Boxer
2. Cairn Terrier
3. Chihuahua
4. Maltese
5. Pug
6. Shetland Sheepdog
7. Toy Poodle
8. Shih Tzu
9. West Highland Terrier
10. Yorkshire Terrier

Breeds Most Susceptible to Seizures

1. American Cocker Spaniel
2. Basset Hound
3. Beagle
4. Border Collie
5. Collie
6. Dachshund
7. Norwich Terrier
8. Pug
9. Poodle
10. Setter (English, Irish)

Most Toxic Plants to Canines

They are right out in your backyard and are potentially lethal to your dog. You may have been cultivating these deadly plants for years without knowing the risk they pose to your favorite four-legged friend.

1. Tomato Vine
2. Rhubarb
3. Skunk Cabbage
4. Daffodil
5. Azalea
6. Delphinium
7. Spinach
8. Peach Tree
9. Jasmine
10. Lily of the Valley

Got Allergies? Here's the Hound for You

Although new research indicates that living with a dog actually helps with allergies, that may not be comforting news if you are suffering from the heavy dander of a dog. There are actually dogs that are "allergy-friendly" and are as easy on a nose as they are on the eyes. Following is a list of the top ten non-shedding, low-dander dogs.

1. BEDLINGTON TERRIER

The breed said to have the heart of a lion but the appearance of a lamb is an aggressive and very effective rodent killer. Developed around 1825 by English miners in an attempt to control the rat population in the mines, the Bedlington is a combination of the Dandi Dinmont, the otterhound, and the whippet. But do not let the sweet lamblike appearance fool you; this can be a temperamental breed.

2. POODLE

Although the exact origin of the poodle remains open to debate (France, Germany, and Denmark claim the rights to this intelligent dog), it is universally agreed the poodle is intelligent, brave, and good-natured. The teacup, toy, miniature, and standard all come in a variety of colors and sizes that accommodate different coat styles to suit the style of their owner. The poodle is used as a companion dog, but (it's a big secret in the dog world) they make great watchdogs.

3. SOFT-COATED WHEATON TERRIER

This breed has a thick coat, but it is noted as a clean, relatively dander-free dog as good for guarding and herding as it is for apartment living. This terrier is the youngest representative of the breed, making its first appearance as late as the 1930s.

4. BICHON FRISE

The bichon frise, a combination of the poodle, the Barbet, and the Irish water spaniel, first appeared in the fourteenth century. Traded by Spanish sailors, the breed became quite popular in sixteenth-century royal courts. Among commoners, the bichon was often seen on the streets as a companion to organ grinders or circus performers. This breed sheds little or no hair.

5. SCHNAUZERS

Whether miniature, standard, or giant, this breed makes as good a watchdog as he does a companion. Intelligent and eager to please, these dogs love to bark. Used in the eighteenth century as carriage dogs and watchdogs in the stables, schnauzers (the word, *schnauze*, is German for muzzle) is also an excellent rodent hunter.

6. BASENJI

An extremely clean dog (and devoid of any odor), this breed is known as the "barkless dog." Basenjis appeared more than five thousand years ago in Egyptian tombs, and they continue to be used as tracking dogs in the forests of Africa and for hunting small game. They are said to be cheerful, loving, and good with children.

7. MALTESE

Once described by the Greek philosopher Theophrastus as belonging to the "Melita" breed, anther word for Malta, the Maltese has always been a companion dog—delicate in features as well as nature. This dog does not do well in dampness and should be kept dry and warm. No dog enjoys being cold and wet, but the Maltese is particularly sensitive to harsh environments and may fall ill. The Maltese does not shed its fur in the spring or fall.

8. SALUKI

This graceful dog, considered to be a gift of Allah, hails from the ancient times. Saluki, named after the Arab city (Salug), is still an avid hunter of gazelles in its native Persia (Iran). This affectionate, good-natured dog is exceptionally clean.

9. TELOMIAN

Very similar to the Basenji in appearance, this ancient breed is raised by Malaysian aborigines where it is used as a hunter, watchdog, and herding dog. Brought to the United States in 1963, it is exclusively thought of as a companion dog—noted for its cleanliness and "happy yodeling."

10. PINSCHER

Thought of as the minipinscher, this breed is delightful-
ly playful, intelligent, and clean. Though small in size,
this breed also makes a marvelous watchdog. Its origins date back to ancient times, but the breed was not
fully recognized until the end of the nineteenth century.
Today, this dog is used mostly for companionship.

HONORABLE MENTION

It must be noted that the rare and hairless Chinese
crested is also noted for its cleanliness. Subject to sunburn and frostbite, this little guy needs to be kept in a
comfortably warm environment. Although the name
would suggest China, many scholars believe its place
of origin is Turkey or Ethiopia. Little is known about
this unusual breed.

Worst People Foods to Feed Your Pup

It's fun to sneak snacks to your dog. Many people give the last couple of bites of whatever they are eating to their puppy, figuring, "if it's good enough for me . . ." But our digestive systems are not the same, and we need to remember that for the sake of our dogs. In other instances, people often give something to their dogs they would never eat themselves. It is important to know that our dogs are susceptible to food poisoning or worse from the very foods we eat.

1. CHOCOLATE

Chocolate contains a compound called theobromine (as well as varying levels of caffeine), which can wreak havoc on a dog's heart and central nervous system. In Virginia, a Samoyed mix had to have her stomach pumped after consuming a bowlful of M&Ms. Reportedly, the vet told her owners that the high toxic content of theobromine and caffeine could have been fatal. Had a smaller breed of dog consumed the same amount of chocolate, his owners might not have been so lucky. A single milk chocolate bar would not be as

233

toxic as a bar of unsweetened baker's chocolate, which contains ten times the amount of theobromine and caffeine. Dogs and chocolate do not mix!

2. TURKEY SKIN

After Thanksgiving dinner, pet owners love to give left-over turkey to their cats and dogs. Although cats are able to digest the turkey's meat and skin, dogs should never be fed the skin; it is toxic to them. Turkey skin can cause pancreatic distress in dogs. Shock, extreme fatigue, vomiting, diarrhea, and, in a few cases, fatality are possible results after serving your pooch turkey skin. Be sure to peel away the skin before serving Fido his feast.

3. CHICKEN OR TURKEY BONES

As with turkey skin, turkey (and chicken) bones can be a real hazard to dogs. So much so that the American Veterinary Medical Association recommends securing the bones in something chewproof when disposing of them in the garbage. Turkey or chicken bones are so small and sharp (when chewed) that they can cause significant internal damage, including piercing or tearing the dog's esophagus.

4. BEEF OR PORK BONES

But these are safe, right? Wrong. The tiny "spicules" or small, sharp pieces of bones that dogs ingest while gnawing away on a beef or pork bone can damage the lining of the their gastrointestinal tract. Just as plumbers advise against putting eggshells in the garbage disposal (they bind together to form a cement-like substance), dog owners are advised against giving beef or pork bones to their dogs. Partial or complete blockage can occur, possibly killing your dog. Or, you may spend hundreds of dollars at the vet, trying to save your pet. The best bones to give your dogs are the synthetic Nylabones found at your local pet store.

5.   RAW OR UNDERCOOKED MEAT

It has long been argued that dogs were man's best friend way back in caveman days when scraps of raw meat were thrown their way. So, why not throw some undercooked or raw meat to your dog now? Two reasons: today's dog, like today's human, no longer consumes live parasites and/or food-borne bacteria. Just as we have evolved from caveman days, so have our digestive systems. This evolution includes our four-legged friends. Second, there are new risks associated with meat. E. coli and salmonella, for example, must be taken very seriously. It is important that meat eaten by humans and dogs be fully cooked.

6.   GREASY FOOD

As we indulge our pets in what seem to be harmless treats, we see a simultaneous trend—canine obesity is on the rise. Just as greasy food has been a problem with people, allowing our pets to lick left over grease or fat can cause significant weight gain and a dangerous inflammation of the pancreas.

7.   ONIONS AND GARLIC

Garlic and onions have high levels of a sulphur compound that may damage red blood cells if consumed in large amounts. Imagine what fried onion rings could do. Don't even think about giving a bite to your pup.

8. MOLDY FOOD

It may seem reasonable that when you clean out your refrigerator, your dog should be allowed to enjoy some of that food rather than just throwing it out. Moldy cheese, soured cottage cheese, moldy meat, bread, or pasta are commonly offered to hopeful pups. Or, if ruined foods are not disposed of properly, a successful trash-digger can ingest them. Believe it or not, moldy food can cause severe reactions in dogs: muscle spasms, tremors or seizures, and, in some rare cases, death.

9. MOLDY WALNUTS

Just as moldy dairy products are dangerous, so are moldy walnuts; they have a toxin know as Penitrem A, which produces a fungus that can cause seizures, tremors, and, in extreme cases, death.

10. SALT

Remember, two grams of salt or half a teaspoon of salt per pound of a dog's body weight can be lethal. While most people food we offer our pets does not contain this much salt, a small dog could be in real danger with a bag of pretzels or peanuts. Additionally, an old remedy requires salt to induce vomiting when poison consumption is feared. This is a remedy that could kill your dog.

Dog Exercises for Year-Round Fun

Spring/Summer Activities

1. Take your dog to a baseball or soccer game—it's a great opportunity for socialization with other canine friends. Soak up all the noises and smells.
2. Teach your dog to play Frisbee. Or, for the more serious athlete, begin training for agility or field competition. Local pet stores have information about different dog clubs in your area.
3. March in a parade.
4. Enter a 10k race—even if you both walk the entire way.
5. Go to a park.
6. Go camping at a public campground. Make sure dogs are permitted and follow any posted rules.
7. Order a cool drink and a cup of ice at an outdoor café and watch the world go by together.
8. Teach your dog to swim—be prepared to jump in!
9. Send your dog to a weeklong camp of doggy day-care.
10. Drive to a different neighborhood and walk around—take in all the new smells and sights.

Fall/Winter

1. Go the pet store and pick out a favorite treat.
2. Rake leaves and hide goodies in different piles—send your dog on his own adventure hunt.
3. Play fetch.
4. Take a brisk early walk on a hiking trail; fall is dogs' favorite time of year!
5. Gather firewood together—and teach him to carry his own firewood! (See Ways to Raise a Happy Puppy: Teach the Most Common Pet Tricks.)
6. Have a snowball fight.
7. Mush! Rig a sled to your puppy—no matter the size—and let him haul something weight-appropriate.
8. Take a car ride on a very cold day with the windows down (with your dog properly restrained).
9. Play hide-and-seek in the house. (See Ways to Raise a Happy Puppy: Teach the Most Common Pet Tricks.)
10. Bundle up and order something hot for you, bring along a chew toy for your dog, and sit outside a café to watch the world slip and slide by.

VI
Finding and Keeping the Perfect Puppy

Bite Prevention Tips for Kids

According to the Humane Society of the United States, dog bites are the number one public health problem for children, outnumbering measles, mumps, and whooping cough combined. With more than 40 percent of all reported dog bites involving children, it is important to teach your children some general safety rules when it comes to dogs. Although much of this was discussed in "Bite Prevention Tips for Joggers," it bears repeating for children.

1. TREAT DOGS WITH RESPECT

Do not tease them by poking a stick through a fence or barking at them. Never provoke them into growling, barking, or lunging at the fence.

2. DO NOT CHASE DOGS OR HAVE THEM CHASE YOU

A game of chase can quickly turn into a hard bite on the bottom.

3.   AVOID STRANGE DOGS, NO MATTER HOW CUTE THEY ARE

Never go on to someone else's property to pet a strange dog.

4.   ALWAYS ASK BEFORE PETTING A STRANGE DOG

A very cute dog sitting quietly by a tree can actually be an aggressive dog who is not properly socialized with children. Or a dog could have an injury you don't know about. If you pet him on a sore spot, he might bite out of pain. Always ask the owner for permission to pet the dog first. If no one is around, stay away from the dog.

5.   DO NOT SCREAM OR RUN AROUND DOGS

High-pitched screaming or fast movements may alarm or frighten a dog, causing him to bite.

6.   RESPECT A DOG'S PRIVACY

Do not bother a dog when he is eating or sleeping. It is also important to remember to leave a dog alone while he is sitting behind a fence (his yard is his room) or in a car.

7.   DO NOT STAND AND STARE AT A DOG

Even the nicest dog might misinterpret this as a threat and act out.

8.   DO NOT STEAL TOYS OR BONES FROM A DOG

These are his things. Leave them alone and respect his property, just as you teach him to respect your things.

9. DO NOT TRY TO BREAK UP A DOGFIGHT

Leave the fight immediately and find an adult. Even your most beloved pet might accidentally bite you should you stick your hand in the middle of a fight.

10. UNDERSTAND THE WARNING SIGNS OF AN ANGRY DOG

Barking, growling, snarling with teeth and/or ears laid flat back are all signs of unhappiness. It is also important to know that a wagging tail can be a sign of aggression! Stiff legs, hair standing up on the back of a dog, and a stiff, tail wagging can be signs of a dog that might bite. Stay calm and quiet and move away slowly.

Golden Rules for Babies and Dogs

Dogs are soft and cuddly and lots of fun to tease and torment. There are plenty of dogs out there who can and will tolerate ear pulls and painful fur removal by sticky fingers, but now is the time to teach your baby about puppy etiquette. By instilling the rules below at an early age, you can save both child and dog a lot of pain and heartache.

1. WHO'S THE BOSS

Dogs think they are equal to small children and do not take kindly to being ordered around by an equal. They are pack animals who view children as members of their pack. Children under the age of ten should not be allowed to give commands or discipline dogs. ("Dog Bite King" attorney Kenneth Phillips suggests that no child under the age of twelve should.)

2. MINE, MINE, MINE . . .

It is important that you begin teaching your dog patience. You should be able to take toys away from your dog without incident. If your dog responds aggressively when you do this, be sure to contact a trainer right away. Having said that, it is equally important that your child not be allowed to crawl over to/walk up to a dog and remove a toy. Each time the child takes the toy away, the dog can become more territorial and think, *Uh oh, here comes the baby!* then guard the toy.

3. WHAT'S FOR DINNER

Your baby or child should not be interested in what Fido is having for dinner. Even the most mild-mannered pup can become alarmed at seeing little fingers creeping into his dog dish and may lash out. While a dog should never be allowed to growl or become possessive about his food, don't push it. Early training with the baby or toddler can prevent any misunderstandings about dinnertime (or a trip to the emergency room).

4. ROUGHHOUSING

Two of the most common reasons for a child being bitten are teasing and rough housing with the dog. Ask a child who has been bitten and she is usually completely perplexed as to why she was. *They were having fun.* Pulling tails, roughhousing, rolling on top of and leaping wildly around dogs is a lot of fun—until the dog gets tired of it.

5. TOP DOG

As busy as you are trying to teach your child not to pull on the dog's ears, you need to watch the dog. Dogs love babies because they are sticky and yummy and have all kinds of delicious things stuck to their bodies. Even better, it's very easy to steal crackers and cheese sticks out of their hands, and they have no other recourse but to cry. Do not allow your dog to view your baby as a feeding ground. When snack time comes, put the two in separate rooms.

6. ADULT SUPERVISION

It should be constant. Babies, toddlers, and small children cannot defend themselves. Even the most kind-hearted dog can become a little too enthusiastic about greeting a baby or playing with the new friend. Occasionally, new babies in the house can cause great jealousy in the four-legged former baby of the house. Be prepared. Be ever present.

7. DOG TIRED

When a dog is sleeping or tired, babies need to understand that he is not to be bothered. Yes, even babies can learn to leave Fido alone when he is sleeping. By teaching small children to respect the needs of the family dog, you will ensure a more empathetic, safer child.

8. SICK OR INJURED

The same rules apply. Babies and toddlers need to understand that a dog—no matter how sweet—will bite when he has an ouch.

9. IN RETREAT

For twenty minutes, a baby has been tormenting the sweetest dog in the world. Finally, disgusted, the dog gets up and leaves the room, hoping to get away from the child. But the child toddles gleefully after the dog. This is a time when many children are snapped at.

Children must be taught to respect the "I've had enough" walk and find something else to play with. Again, this can be taught at a very young age. Most family dogs try to get away before they feel forced to snap or bite.

10. ENDLESS LOVE

Once the guidelines are understood between children and dogs (and even then, adults should always be present), an incredible bond can form between the two. Children benefit greatly from having a dog friend. They are more generous, sensitive, gentle, and giving in nature than any human friend your child will ever have. In return, dogs become more trusting and patient when they have human pals. It is a win/win situation that can be enhanced by your diligence and training. Good luck.

Reasons to Crate Your Puppy

Many people think crating is cruel when, in truth, it is one of the kindest things you can do for your puppy. And, he will come to love the sense of security.

1. SECURITY FOR YOU

Knowing that your puppy isn't destroying the house while you are sitting in traffic is a great relief. You can relax and enjoy seeing your puppy when you get home. One of the number one complaints dog trainers hear is that the puppy cowers when the owner comes home. Because the puppy has made one or multiple mistakes, the owner instantly (and wrongly) punishes the puppy. Now a pattern has been established: Owner comes home, dog cowers and is punished but has no idea why. Your puppy forgot about the destruction he caused four hours ago. For this reason, everyone is happier when his chances of making a mistake are limited.

2. SECURITY FOR THE DOG

The crate is a huge security blanket for pups. While you are away, the pup lies in his crate, sleeping much of the time, awaiting your return. The crate becomes a place of comfort. As you use the crate more often, you will see that when there is lightning and thunder, the puppy sees his crate as the perfect shelter.

3. SAFETY FOR THE PUPPY

In addition to security, the crate is a safety factor as well. Many puppies have been killed while chewing on exposed television or computer cables. If you eliminate the chance that they will get into trouble, you ensure their safety while you are gone.

4. HOUSEBREAKING

If you stick to a strict feeding, watering, and walking schedule, the crate can be your best friend while housebreaking your puppy. Dogs do not like to relieve themselves in their small "area," and they will learn to wait until you come home to let them outside. As soon as you get home, open the door to the crate and immediately take your puppy outside. Do not express too much excitement when you get home because it might be too difficult for your wildly happy puppy to contain himself. As soon as you are outside, heap praise and love on your puppy—he can let loose there.

5. DESTRUCTIVE BEHAVIOR

Just as with housebreaking, the crate will help train your puppy not to chew when he is teething or bored. As your puppy grows older and becomes more responsible, you can give him more time to roam the house, but he must earn the right to have free rein. In the meantime, the crate is the ideal training tool for a puppy, or an immature adult dog who is adjusting to a new home.

6. WHEN THERE ARE TWO

The crate is especially needed if there is more than one puppy in the house! What one puppy won't think of, the other one will, and the destruction is double. By separating and crating the two dogs, they will learn to have play time when they are out and sleep while you are gone. This is a behavior you hope will carry over into adulthood when they are normally loose in the house. You need to have two different crates for two different puppies.

7. TRAVELING SAFELY

Whether your dog is flying in a plane or is a backseat passenger in your car, crating ensures safety and comfort while traveling. Once he learns to sit or sleep quietly in his crate, traveling becomes much less stressful for him. You'll be the one worrying, not your dog.

8. SICK AS A DOG

Should your puppy become injured or ill, the last thing you want is for him to be terrified of being crated or caged at the vet. If he can remain calm inside the cage, the healing process will go much more quickly and quietly.

9. IN CASE OF EMERGENCY

Should you become ill or injured and your puppy must be crated, you will have peace of mind knowing that he is not stressed. His crate is essentially his room and will give him more security while you are away.

10. THE ROOM

Best of all, as your puppy matures and graduates from the crate, he will return to his little room in the middle of the day just to take a nap or to chew a favorite toy. By leaving the crate out (with the door open), you allow him to move in and out of his crate at will throughout the day.

Ways *not* to Use the Crate

1. PUNISHMENT

Never use the crate as a form of punishment. Although it is tempting to put your puppy or dog in the crate while cleaning up a mess he just made, it should never be viewed as a form of punishment by you or your dog. His crate is his room—a place of comfort and security. New problems will develop if your dog sees his crate as a negative (and frightening) place.

2. DON'T *NOT* USE YOUR CRATE

This can't be said enough—you must use the crate. So often owners purchase a crate, talk to trainers and read all the proper materials regarding crate training and, upon seeing it, decide their puppy is much happier without one. Crate training is an essential tool in housebreaking. If you ignore the crate, you may delay your puppy's progress and punish him needlessly. Your pet will be happier with the crate in the long run because it will become a place of comfort and the perfect tool for housebreaking and basic obedience.

3. DON'T KEEP YOUR DOG IN THE CRATE TOO LONG

Excessive use of a crate can cause emotional problems for your puppy, including eating his own feces, urinating on himself (and sleeping in it), shyness, and withdrawal. While the debate continues among dog trainers and behaviorists about how long is too long—some argue no more than four hours a day, others argue no more than eight—all agree that eight hours is the limit. In the middle of that eight-hour stint—the typical workday—it is still important to have someone let the puppy out to go to the bathroom, drink, and eat lunch. Set up a time in the middle of the day when a dog walker, neighbor, babysitter, or older child can let the puppy out. Remember, it takes a village to raise a puppy.

4. USING THE CRATE DAY AND NIGHT

This is a huge no-no. Many new owners understand that they are not to use the crate more than eight hours at a time. Serious problems can occur with a dog who's been crated for four-plus-hour stints day and night. You have to choose which time of day he needs to be crated. For working families, the most popular schedule is to crate the pup during the day when no one is home. At night, while everyone is sleeping, the young dog can be kept in one room with an adult, using a baby gate to keep him in so he has room to move around and be social but not be "locked up." It is one or the other.

5. PUTTING TWO DOGS TOGETHER

Although it seems like a great idea to put two small puppies in the same crate, don't. (This is assuming the puppies are more than ten weeks old.) Two pups in the

same crate increase the likelihood for urination/defe-
cation in the crate, which will hinder the housebreaking process. If you invest in a second crate, the pups
will learn to rest comfortably while they are in their
"rooms."

6. DON'T CONTINUE TO CRATE IF THE PUP IS AFRAID

You may have to rethink how you have been using the
crate if your pup is afraid of it. It is wise to contact a
trainer/canine behaviorist to determine the problem
and learn how to retrain your puppy. He must learn to
think of his crate in the most positive light. Proper
puppy training will fix this problem, but do not continue shoving him into the crate kicking and screaming.
Address the problem.

7. DON'T ALLOW CHILDREN TO CLIMB INTO THE CRATE

This is your dog's room and must be respected as
such. Allowing a child in the crate can create territorial issues with aggressive tendencies. Make it known
that the dog's crate is off-limits to anyone and everyone, except the family dog.

8. DON'T ALLOW CHILDREN IN THE CRATE WHILE YOUR DOG IS INSIDE

Just as with 7, above, keep children out for everyone's
safety. It may be a nonissue, but you don't want to find
out the hard way that your dog is territorial.

9. DON'T SHUT THE DOOR

While your puppy is free in the house, be sure to leave
the crate door open so that he can go in and out as he
chooses. This will help create the "room" feeling about
the crate. It is a good sign when your puppy walks into

his crate, sniffs around, and walks back out. Just leave the door open.

10. DON'T STOP TOO SOON

The biggest mistake most new dog owners make is to stop crating too soon. Often it seems pups/young adults have grasped the housebreaking/destructive rules well enough and the crate is put away, only to discover that accidents are occur more frequently. Most trainers suggest crating a dog past the first year before giving him full-time free run of the house.

Things to Ask
a Breeder

You've decided on the breed you want and are very excited about purchasing your brand-new puppy. You even have the name picked out! But rushing to buy a puppy is one of the biggest mistakes people make. There are ten questions you must ask the breeder, not only to learn more about the kind of dog you have chosen but, more important, to find out the kind of breeder you are buying from. Temperament, medical issues, and finances hinge on the following questions.

1. HOW LONG HAS THE BREEDER BEEN INVOLVED WITH THIS BREED?

This is a key issue. Be wary of anyone who is selling his or her first litter of puppies. The breeder can be super-nice, but it doesn't mean the breeder knows what he or she is doing. Ask if the breeder has worked with other breeds as well. It's common for well-known, well-established breeders to invest in two or three different breeds, but if you find someone who has been involved with the "it" breeds—the popular ones—strictly as a way of making money, beware!

2. WHAT'S THE DOWNSIDE TO THIS BREED?

Every good breeder can provide a long list of the congenital defects of his or her breed. If the breeder knows his or her business and has been paying attention, the person is well aware of the problems specific breed faces and isn't afraid to share that information with you. Truly good breeders are interested in providing better, stronger puppies and are willing to discuss any problems their dogs have. Know this: every breed has problems! Be wary of anyone who says otherwise.

3. HOW IS THE BREEDER WORKING WITH THE BREED?

Another good question. A good breeder will be personally invested in better health and nutrition for his or her dogs. When the breeder can discuss having the dogs tested or screened for hip dysplasia, for example, this is a very good sign. Ask the breeder about long-term plans for the dogs he or she breeds.

4. WHERE ARE THE CANINE PARENTS?

Seeing both parents is helpful in several ways. It allows you to see the condition and overall physique of the dogs as well as how they behave. Aggressive or unruly parents may be a red flag. More important, you may see how the owners interact with the parents. They should be able to tell you honestly the pros and cons of their adult dogs. Because they want to make sure you are happy with your puppy, they should not be giving the hard sell. They will want you to know, for example, that the mother is a barker or is shy around strangers.

5. WHAT'S THE DOG'S PEDIGREE?

Breeders should also be able to show you a solid line family history—the pedigree—and respond convincingly to any questions you have. Who is who, and what do the titles mean? Do not be afraid to ask.

6. WHERE DO THE PUPPIES LIVE/SLEEP?

Often when puppy-owners-to-be arrive, the puppies are outside, frolicking and looking cute. But it is important to see where and how the puppies spend most of their time. Many puppies are kept in crates or in the basement, where they lack socialization and proper care. This is not what you want. You want the puppies to live everywhere.

7. ARE THESE SHOW DOGS?

There is a difference between show dogs and pets. Just because your puppy has a stunning pedigree does not mean he is show dog material. Something as minor as an overbite can be a very big deal. You need to know whether the puppies have been evaluated and to understand the quality of pup you are considering. A good breeder will not sell you a pet with a show dog price.

8. DOES THE BREEDER OFFER ANY GUARANTEES?

Reputable breeders will guarantee the dog (essentially the pedigree) they are selling you and are willing to guarantee the health and quality of their puppies. Get such a guarantee in writing. Be willing to ask about breeder contracts. Reputable breeders have a vested interest in all their dogs and will want to discuss breeding possibilities or insist on a spay/neuter agreement.

9. **DOES THE BREEDER HAVE REFERENCES?**

This is the one thing most owners are always too embarrassed to ask for. It seems rude. In truth, reputable breeders want and expect you to ask. They are proud of their puppies/kennel and like to spread the word. Before you agree to buy a pup, ask for references and check them out. Guarantees and pedigrees are one thing, checking references out is another.

10. **WHEN CAN I TAKE MY PUPPY HOME?**

Veterinarians, animal behaviorists, and dog trainers never like to see a puppy go home before ten to twelve weeks. Although a breeder might tell you a pup is ready at six or eight weeks, that extra two weeks of socialization with his mother and pack are vital. A breeder who lets pups go before ten weeks should raise a red flag.

When to Walk Away from a Breeder

1. **WHAT'S IN A BREED?**

The expression, "backyard breeders," identifies people who know very little about their breed except that they like them and think they are pretty or handsome. This isn't enough knowledge to help the breed. If your breeder lacks knowledge about the breed, its origins, and its problems, you have to pass.

2. **WHAT DEFECTS?**

Again, your breeder should be able to speak knowledgeably about the problems of his or her specific breed. What congenital defects do the dogs have? Hint: You already know there has to be something because you checked on the Internet or at the library.

3. **THERE ARE NO DEFECTS**

A serious warning sign is the breeder who insists that there is nothing wrong with the breed. Good breeders will want you to be aware of all the potential problems so that you will be prepared and know how to handle them.

4.   IF THEY ARE ONLY BREEDERS

Today's top breeders are extremely busy people; they are involved in various dog clubs, sporting events, and/or dog activities. They know that the more they are involved in the dog community, the more knowledgeable they will become. Additionally, this is how they earn titles and championships for their dogs. Be wary of a breeder who is not involved in the dog community. Remember that the breeder's involvement in the dog community is a way to check up on his or her credentials.

5.   NO LOOKING, PLEASE

Unbelievably, there are "breeders" who do not wish to have people meet and visit with the parents of the litter in question. This is a red flag. You need to see how the dogs look and act before buying.

6.   NO DOCUMENTATION

Simply put, if you are paying the "asking rate" for a specific breed, you need to see the proper paperwork (registrations forms and pedigrees) for the dog. You have a right to receive documentation that matches the quality claimed for the puppy you are buying.

7.   NO SOCIALIZATION

You do not want a puppy who has lived in virtual isolation. Behavioral problems such as aggression, extreme shyness, and nervousness all stem from lack of proper socialization. Trainers can always spot dogs who have lived in isolation right away—they are afraid of anything new or loud. You want a dog that has seen it all.

8.   NO REFERRALS

Once you gather the nerve to ask for referrals, get them. Too many times owners report they were promised referrals but didn't insist on them. Insist! Find out first who you are dealing with because your puppy-to-be can't tell you.

9.   THE EARLY SEND-OFF

Any breeder who is willing to sell a pup under the age of eight weeks is questionable. A sure sign that this is a breeder-for-profit only is his or her agreement to let a puppy leave too soon. The ideal age is ten to twelve weeks—no sooner.

10.   NO QUESTIONS ASKED

Just as you ask questions about the breeder, he or she should ask questions about you. A good breeder wants to know that the puppy is going to a good home and will be inclined to ask about your home, family life, exercise routine, and backyard as well as daily routine, including what you intend to feed the dog and how. If the breeder doesn't ask, be concerned. Again, because they are fully invested in their dogs, good breeders want to know that their pup is in good hands. Many breeders have a contract that stipulates, should you have to give the dog away, it goes back to the breeder.

Things You Should Know about Your Pup from the Animal Shelter

Rescued dogs are the best dogs in the world. They are wonderful with children and other dogs, and they seem to understand that you saved them. They give back love and companionship to you tenfold. That's the best-case scenario. There are, however, plenty of stories of rescues gone bad. Following are ten tips for finding the right dog at the animal shelter.

1. ASK QUESTIONS

Impulse buying is never a good idea, and when looking for a dog, it is unfair to both you and the puppy. You need to make sure your prospective puppy fits into your lifestyle. A hyperactive dog with a history of running away, for example, should not be expected to live in an apartment with little exercise. Dogs exhibiting signs of fear or aggression should not be exposed to children without prior professional consultation. Talk to a handler about the dog's background and behaviors before finalizing your decision. Just because the puppy looks cute does not mean he will do well in your home.

2. THE AGE OF YOUR PUP

The reality is that puppies move very quickly from the animal shelter, so you are most likely to get an older puppy. The average adoptive age for shelter puppies is between six and ten months. The good news is that, at that age, you can begin basic obedience training right away. This will enhance the house rules you are trying to instill in your new family member, making everyone (including the puppy) happier.

3. OLDER DOGS, OLD HABITS

Older dogs may have habits you do not like. Many older dogs are in the shelter because their former owners could not deal with behavioral problems such as digging, barking, or wetting in the house. More often than not, the behavioral problems are not that bad, and with patience, time, and training, an older dog can be the best dog. This is why it is standard practice for Hollywood animal trainers to visit animal shelters to look for new canine and feline stars. With a little tweaking, a star can be born! Perhaps the dogs work so hard and are successful because they are so grateful that they were rescued.

4. TAKE A WALK

Today, most animal shelters have an outdoor facility where you can go outside and spend time with the dog or dogs in which you are interested. For your walk, bring along a squeaky toy and/or a ball. When you are outside, let the pup explore the area first. Once he has settled down, squeak the toy and notice how interested and responsive he is. You want a dog who is curious and eager to play but not too roughly. When the toys are out of sight, you should be able to make small noises with your mouth to encourage the puppy to come to you. Again, it does not matter how cute the puppy is; you need to avoid the dog who cringes in the corner or shies away from your hand.

5. WHAT YOU SEE IS NOT WHAT YOU GET

"He was so good when I got him! Now all he does is bark and tear everything apart." This is one of the most common complaints dog trainers hear from new owners. Because most dogs in the animal shelter spend twenty-three to twenty-three and a half hours a day in a small kennel, their behavior is often quite different from when they are comfortable in their new homes. Typically, there is a two- to three-week grace period during which the dog is still feeling his way in the new house. As the dog becomes more comfortable, he may begin to chew or bark, which is the very thing that landed him in the shelter in the first place. If you are alert for signs of changing behavior, you can stop them before they get started. (See the chapters "Most Common Behavior Problems (and Quick Tips to Fix Them)" and "The AKC-Approved Good Citizen Test: Questions to Determine If Your Dog Is a Good Citizen.")

6. TOP DOG

The sooner you establish yourself as the pack leader, the easier your dog's transition from animal shelter to house will be. Be ready to use the crate and begin basic obedience as soon as possible. By teaching your pet basic obedience, you will establish yourself as leader, learn how to better communicate with your dog, give him a physical outlet for his energy, and build his confidence. Remember, your new pound puppy may be feeling very nervous and insecure. As he learns to trust you and enjoy making you happy, everything else will fall into place.

7. **PREPARING THE HOUSE**

Make your list and check it twice. Before you bring the new puppy or dog home, be sure you have all the equipment you need: crate, leash, training and flat collars, ID tag, food, toys, the name and appointment date and time with a veterinarian, and a trainer. And, as you would do for a human child, ensure that tempting and/or breakable possessions are out of the dog's reach.

8. **MAKING UP FOR LOST TIME**

Many new owners feel so badly about the terrible life their puppy had before he came to their own home that they want to give him everything: new toys, new friends, and lots and lots of food. All of this can be a shock to the dog's system. He needs to have quiet time to explore his new home and surroundings and should not be introduced to new things and food too quickly. Goodies, rawhides, even a different brand of dog food can cause diarrhea. Your new dog is very happy to be with you and doesn't need all the fancy bells and whistles (and people food). Basic obedience, love, and patience are his best friend.

9. **REPEAT OFFENDERS**

There seem to be too many dogs in the world and too few adoptive homes, but one of the biggest problems at animal shelters is getting repeat offenders, that is, people who refuse to have their animals spayed or neutered and continue to bring in litters of pups, expecting the shelter to act as a broker in the puppy-selling business. While puppies are adopted out more successfully, this means other dogs may not find a home. If you know anyone who uses a shelter as a puppy broker, offer to have his or her animal spayed, talk to local vets about a payment program, or appeal to the person's responsibilities as a dog owner.

According to the Humane Society of the United States, an unspayed female dog can be responsible for producing sixty-seven thousand dogs in six years. Every five minutes, more than two dozen dogs are euthanized in the United States. An animal shelter should never be considered a dropping-off place for dogs: We can all make a difference in our communities by trying to convince friends and neighbors to neuter their pets.

10. THE FOOLPROOF PLAN

The best way to find the puppy or dog of your dreams is to donate a little of your time to walk dogs at your local animal shelter. Offer one or two hours a week at the shelter. Not only will you be providing a wonderful service to dogs in need, allowing them to stretch their legs and sniff the big, wide world, but you will also learn a little more about the dogs who might join your family. Many times, volunteers wind up adopting a dog they had not even considered in the beginning. And, of course, when you are more confident about your choice of pet, both of you will be happier.

Things You Should Ask Yourself Before You Get a Dog

If you have not yet picked out a dog, there are some important issues you need to consider and discuss with your family. Too often people choose a breed because of the way it looks, without considering how (or when) a dog of that breed will fit their lifestyle. Here are ten things you need to ask yourself.

1. ARE YOU READY FOR A DOG?

Every day, throughout the United States, unwanted dogs appear in animal shelters because they simply don't fit into the family plan. People get dogs for a variety of reasons, and while it seemed like a good idea to get a dog, it may turn out that there really isn't enough time in the day to play, train, and bond with the puppy. Before long, the puppy is a dog without manners or social skills. Owning a dog means no longer staying out all night, going away for weekends, or pulling all-nighters at work. Once you become a dog owner, you are a responsible member (leader) of a pack and are needed. The payoffs are plentiful, but you must be willing to invest time (and love) in your dog.

2.   IMAGE IS EVERYTHING?

Is your dog a status symbol? Are you looking for a macho dog because it's cool? A foo-foo dog because you loved the movie *Legally Blonde*? The biggest mistake dog owners make is picking a dog because of his appearance rather than his personality. You know the expression, beauty is only skin deep? Well, that includes fur!

3.   ALLERGIES

Of course, we know that dogs may actually help fight allergies (see the chapter, "Got Allergies? Here's the Hound for You: Best Breeds for Owners with Allergies"), but there are those who suffer specifically because of animal hair. If you really want a dog (we don't blame you!), be reasonable. Don't buy a dog with a thick undercoat or one that sheds year-round. Give yourself and your sinuses a break; talk to your vet before choosing a breed. Remember, this is a dog you hope to have around for years.

4.   DOGS AND CHILDREN

You have a rough-and-tumble three-year-old. Do you really think getting a Lhaso apso or Maltese is a good idea? Take a hard look at the children who live in your house or even those who come to visit frequently (nieces and nephews) and choose wisely. Hyperactive, loud, rough children are best suited for Labradors, for example. Consider that the group of people most often bitten is five-year-old girls. They love to get into the face of puppy dogs and love them. The puppy may not feel the same way.

A boy's best friend. Labradors are very tolerant
of children's hijinx and roughhousing.

5. OTHER ANIMALS IN THE HOUSE

You have an older dog who suffers from arthritis, and
you've decided to bring a ninety-pound, Newfound
land puppy full of life into the home. You have a cat
who despises dogs or a dog who has been known to
get into fights with other dogs. You are considering
having two unneutered males in the house. You need

to pick and choose your new breed carefully. Speak with your vet and/or a trainer before introducing the new puppy.

6. GROOMING CONSIDERATIONS

Grooming your dog involves two things: time and money. This is especially true of breeds like the Lhaso apso, shih tzu, poodle, schnauzer, cocker spaniel, Yorkshire terrier, and Shetland sheepdog, to name a few. They need professional grooming about every eight weeks. The cost can be double for larger breeds like the giant schnauzer, Old English sheepdog, chow chow, Great Pyrenees, Samoyed, collie, and Afghan hound.

7. CLIMATE CONSIDERATIONS

It would seem obvious that the climate where you live would and should influence what kind of breed you choose. However, many people are so taken with the look of a dog that they do not consider the heat or cold factor. A Saint Bernard in the Louisiana bayou or a Chihuahua in Siberia really doesn't make sense. Think about the comfort of the animal before bringing him home.

8. CAN YOU AFFORD A DOG?

Providing that you have a healthy dog, you can reasonably estimate two veterinary visits per year; the cost of good-quality dog food, treats, toys, leash/collar provisions, flea/tick medications, possible grooming costs, and obedience training; and the occasional need for boarding or pet sitting. This does not include the cost of the actual dog should you decide to purchase one with an excellent pedigree. You have to answer this question honestly for everyone's sake.

Avoiding veterinary bills, could expose your dog to all kinds of risks, including heartworms. Good-quality dog food will prolong your dog's life, making him healthier and happier. Bottom line: there are costs associated with a healthy/happy dog that you must be willing to except.

9. RECEIVING A PUPPY AS A GIFT

The cute puppy as Christmas gift—this is a difficult situation because if the puppy does not fit into your life, how do you return him? Animal behaviorists have the answer: find the puppy a new home. It is better to find the puppy a loving home in which he will be welcomed rather than to have the puppy become attached and then give him away. It is better to wound (slightly) the ego of the gift giver than to raise an unhappy dog.

10. GIVING A PUPPY AS A GIFT

In considering 9, above, be sure that you really know if the intended recipient really wants and needs a dog. Ask yourself if the kind of breed or temperament of the animal and the lifestyle of the person will work before bringing the two together. Make this present the best gift ever: include free puppy training classes!

VII
Looking for Help

Moving with
Your Dog

Moving can be one of the most stressful times in your life, not to mention your pup's. This is a time when many dogs run away or are lost. Confused by all the disruption, packing, and foot traffic, many dogs simply disappear. But moving can also be a happy, stress-free period for your dog. Here are some tips to help ensure a safe and happy trip for you both.

1. PACKING THE HOUSE

As the process of moving begins, be sure to keep your dog's routine as normal as possible. He will see boxes moving about and will certainly feel your stress, but if you keep his feeding, walking, and play schedules the same, he will feel more secure. The most common mistake is ignoring the dog. After all, so much more is going on, it's hard to keep up with him and his needs. But these are the times he will simply find entertainment or attention somewhere else or become destructive out of nervousness. This is also a time when doors are left open, and dogs take themselves for a walk. Try to pay more attention to your dog. If the event is too stressful or small children are involved, you may want to ask a friend to keep your dog while you pack.

2. PACKING THE SUITCASE

Again, keep the routine as normal as possible. Many dogs recognize the sight of a suitcase as the sign they will be boarded. Great anxiety can be associated with the suitcase. If this is your dog, pack while he is outside. Arrange for someone else to take him for a long walk while you pack.

3. TRAVELING BY CAR

If you are traveling by car, be sure to pack a dog-friendly car. Have food, water, and toys easily accessible, and be prepared for a breakdown. Should you be stranded on the side of the highway, your dog should have a proper-fitting collar and leash and an ample supply of water.

Finding a hotel may be another issue, particularly if you are traveling with a larger breed. Vacationing with Your Pet by Eileen Barish (Pet Friendly Publications, 800-638-3637) is an excellent resource for all U.S. hotels and motels that accept dogs.

4. CARSICKNESS

Many dogs love to travel by car, but some do get carsick. Be sure not to feed or water your dog just before going on a long trip, and give him plenty of time to go to the bathroom before loading him into the car.

If carsickness is already an issue, "practicing" the big move well before the actual date can help. Begin with short, relatively easy trips, slowly increasing the time frame so that he gets adjusted to longer and longer trips. If the carsickness persists, talk to your vet about motion sickness; a stomach-calming medication may help.

5. TRAVELING BY PLANE

As soon as you know you are flying, be sure to contact the airlines. Every airline has different policies about animals, including sizes and breeds. Consider the time of year you are traveling, how long your dog might be on the tarmac, and your dog's comfort. Introducing your dog to the crate just three minutes before boarding is unfair to Fido. Practice getting him into and out of a crate and make sure it is the right size (he should be able to stand up and do a full circle inside) and he is comfortable with the crate before traveling.

Proper identification of your dog and any special medical needs must placed plainly on the outside of the crate as well as on his collar. Anyone see Homeward Bound II? Two dogs and a cat escape from their crates on the tarmac. Although this movie had a Hollywood ending, not all dogs and cats are that lucky.

6. MEDICAL RECORDS

Traveling with medical records is a must. Do not wait until you have moved to your new city or town to send for your dog's records; plan in advance. As soon as you know you are moving (and where), discuss the move with your vet and ask for recommendations in the new city. If you can, be sure to have a veterinarian contact in your new city should something happen when you move in. If you have your dog's records on hand, you will be ready.

7. BE PREPARED FOR A DIFFERENT PERSONALITY

During the move, discourage strange dogs from playing with your dog at rest stops or allowing strangers to get kissy-wissy in his face. Many travelers ask, "Is it my imagination or is my dog depressed?" It is possible. Many travel-weary dogs become irritable, depressed, and/or confused. Although it is difficult to keep his schedule the same while you are on the road, you should try to feed him at the same time and continue to take him on long walks at the end of the day. If you keep his tummy on schedule and give him regular exercise, he will be a happier traveler.

8. COMFORT TOYS

Security blankets, favorite toys, and/or bones are very important. Just as he sees you packing up your worldly possessions, he needs to see that his are coming along as well. For added security, give him an old (worn) shirt of yours that he can snuggle up to during the drive/flight. It smells like you, which will comfort him.

9. UNPACKING IN THE NEW HOME

This transition is even more dangerous than the initial move. While he was confused by all the packing at his old house, the environment was still familiar to him. In the new home/new town, everything is strange, new, exciting—and dangerous. He might bolt from fear or strike out on an adventure only to become lost. Be sure, as movers are walking in and out of the house, that there is no way for him to escape. And no matter how tired you are that first night in your new home, snap on a leash and take him for a walk in his new neighborhood.

10. THE NEW ENVIRONMENT

Learn all about the new environment as quickly as you can. Each city or town has its own leash laws, friendly and unfriendly dogs, parks, and even diseases to learn about. Most important, find out who the neighborhood dogs are. It will be helpful to know whom to avoid.

Top Canine Organizations for Charity, Assistance Dogs, and/or Love

When we read stories about dogs like Lucas, the search and rescue dog, we understand the limitations of our own dogs but love them unconditionally. The truth is, most dogs have triple the potential we give them credit for. But not every dog can be a Lassie or a Lucas. While Lassie is rescuing children from burning buildings, and Lucas is sniffing out disaster victims, most of our dogs couldn't find a sock in a pile of laundry. All the more reason for us to admire and appreciate the efforts of those—both two- and four-legged—who have devoted so much of their time and energy to great causes. If you want to learn more, volunteer, offer financial support, or raise a puppy, there are some great contacts for you.

1. AKC CANINE HEALTH FOUNDATION

Dedicated to improving the quality of life for dogs and their owners, this Web site offers everything you need to know about—or helps you find the links to—dog health, proper grooming, training, dogs shows, and more.

American Kennel Club Canine Health Foundation
P.O. Box 37941
Raleigh, NC 27627
888-682-9696
E-mail: akcchf@aol.com
Web site: www.akcchf.org

2. AMERICAN VETERINARY MEDICAL FOUNDATION

This organization is dedicated to helping veterinarians help animals. By providing almost $1 million to various organizations and individuals, the AVMF is able to give back to animal research, animal disaster relief, and veterinarian financial assistance.

American Veterinary Medical Foundation
1931 N. Meacham Road, Suite 1
Schaumburg, IL 60173
800-248-2862 ext. 4355
E-mail: avmf@avma.org
Web site: www.avmf.org

3. CANINE COMPANIONS FOR INDEPENDENCE

A nonprofit organization, Canine Companions works to enhance the lives of people with disabilities by offering highly trained assistance dogs and ongoing support to ensure these dogs and their people are happy.

Canine Companions for Independence
P.O. Box 446
Santa Rosa, CA 95402-0446
800-572-BARK
866-CCI-DOGS
Web site: www.caninecompanions.org

4. **DELTA SOCIETY**

This is the human-animal health connection that offers information on therapy dogs and all the health benefits dogs have to offer. This is a great resource to find all kinds of animal information.

Delta Society
580 Naches Avenue, SW
Suite 101
Renton, WA 98055-2297
425-226-7357
E-mail: info@deltasociety.org
Web site: www.deltasociety.org

5. **GUIDE DOGS FOR THE BLIND**

A nonprofit organization that provides a great service to visually impaired people throughout the United States and Canada, Guide Dogs for the Blind was established in 1942. This organization matches people with guide dogs with the purpose of improving lives.

Guide Dogs for the Blind
P.O. Box 151200
San Rafael, CA 94915-1200
800-295-4050
Web site: www.guidedogs.com

Also:

Guiding Eyes for the Blind
611 Granite Springs Road
Yorktown Heights, NY 10598
800-942-0149
Web site: www.guiding-eyes.org

6. DOGS FOR THE DEAF

This organization chooses dogs from the shelter, taking "unwanted" dogs to train as assistant dogs for the deaf. Their only criterion is that the dogs, usually mixed breeds, must be friendly, energetic, healthy, and intelligent. Taking small to medium-size dogs, no more than two years old, Dogs for the Deaf is making a world of difference for humans and dogs.

Dogs for the Deaf, Inc.
10175 Wheeler Road
Central Point, OR 97502
541-826-9220
Web site: www.dogsforthedeaf.org

7. MORRIS ANIMAL FOUNDATION

The foundation was established in 1955 to honor those students who pursue higher education in animal health, including those who have gone on to get their doctorates in veterinary medicine.

Morris Animal Foundation
45 Inverness Drive East
Englewood, CO 80112
800-243-2345
Web site: www.morrisanimalfoundation.org

8. DORIS DAY ANIMAL LEAGUE

This nonprofit organization focuses on the treatment of animals. The League offers information about health, medical issues, animals in the news, and treatment of animals around the world.

Doris Day Animal League
227 Massachusetts Avenue, NE
Suite 100

Washington, DC 20002
202-546-1761
E-mail: info@ddal.org
Web site: www.ddal.org

9. FRIENDS OF ANIMALS

This nonprofit organization began in 1957 with the mission of protecting animals from cruelty, abuse, and/or neglect. With your donations, more work can be done around the globe to protect our precious animals.

Friends of Animals
777 Post Road, Suite 205
Darien, CT 06820
203-656-1522
Web site: www.friendsofanimals.org

10. HUMANE SOCIETY

The Humane Society of the United States has a wonderful Web site for the entire family to learn more about animals and how to care for and train them. Loaded with fun facts, this site offers pet care galore.

Humane Society of the United States
2100 L Street, NW
Washington, D.C. 20037
202-452-1100
Web site: www.hsus.org

HONORABLE MENTION: KID LINK FOR THE FAMILY

The American Society for the Prevention of Cruelty to Animals has a great site for kids, including a parent guide. Good stuff.

American Society for the Prevention of Cruelty to Animals
424 E. 92nd Street
New York, NY 10128-6804
212-876-7700
Web site: www.animaland.org

Why Does My Dog Do That?

Check the Web to Ask a Trainer

1. Animal Behavior Society
   www.animalbehavior.org
2. Association of Pet Dog Trainers
   www.apdt.com
3. National Association of Dog Obedience
      Instructors, Inc.
   www.nadoi.org
4. The Dogpatch
   www.dogpatch.org
5. Raising Your Dog with the Monks of New Skete
   www.dogsbestfriend.com
6. Pet Behavior Resources
   www.webtrail.com/petbehavior
7. American Dog Trainers Network
   www.inch.com/~dogs
8. www.animaland.org
9. Natural Holistic Health Care
   www.naturalholistic.com
10. American Veterinary Medical Association
   www.avma.org

Top Veterinary Groups

1. American Veterinarian Medical Association
   www.avma.org
2. Canadian Veterinarian Medical Association
   www.crma-acmv.org
3. American Animal Hospital
   www.aahanet.org
4. American College of Veterinary Internal Medicine
   www.acvim.org
5. Orthopedic Foundation for Animals
   www.offa.org
6. PennHip
   www.synbiotics.com
7. Canine Eyes Registration Foundation
   www.vet.purdue.edu/~yshen/cerf.html
8. National Animal Control Center for Poison
   www.prodogs.com
9. U.S. Food and Drug Administration Center for
   Veterinary Medicine
   www.fda.gov/cvm
10. Texas A&M University Veterinary School
    www.cvm.tamu.edu

Clubs to Join with Your Dog

1. **AMERICAN KENNEL CLUB**

5580 Centerview Drive, Suite 200
Raleigh, NC 27606-3390
www.akc.org
In its mission statement, the AKC explains that it maintains a registry for purebred dogs and sanctions dog events, preserving the integrity of canines and breeders. But it is also a marvelous resource guide for researching breeds, breeding, shows, and canine health and happiness.

2. **AMERICAN RESCUE DOG ASSOCIATION**

P.O. Box 151
Chester, NY 10918
www.ardainc.org
The nation's oldest air scenting search dog organization was established in 1972, using German shepherds in missing person cases and natural disasters. In 1982, ARDA created the first national SAR Dog Directory for the National Association for Search and Rescue. If you

are interested in learning more about rescue work with dogs, contact this amazing organization.

3. NATIONAL ASSOCIATION FOR SEARCH AND RESCUE

4500 Southgate Place, Suite 100
Chantilly, VA 20151
703-222-6283
www.nasar.org

To learn more about how you can help fund the working human/canine teams or become part of a search and rescue team, write to NASAR or log on to its Web site, which has a fascinating newsletter, kids corner, and FAQs.

4. NORTH AMERICAN DOG AGILITY COUNCIL

HCR 2, Box 277
St. Maries, ID 83861
www.nadac.com

This is an excellent resource for different clubs and how to train and compete. With exciting information about awards, championships, and national titles, this is a great way to have fun as a spectator or competitor.

5. NORTH AMERICAN FLYBALL ASSOCIATION (NAFA)

1400 Devon Avenue
Chicago, IL 60660

6. UNITED STATES DOG AGILITY ASSOCIATION (USDAA)

P.O. Box 850955
Richardson, TX 75085
214-231-9700
www.usdaa.com

Whether you want to pull up a chair or compete in the Dog Agility Steeplechase, the USDAA can provide a thorough list of dates, places, and required qualifications for you and your canine competitor.

7. WORLD CANINE FREESTYLE ORGANIZATION, LTD. (WCFO)

P.O. Box 350122
Brooklyn, NY 11235
718-332-8336
www.worldcaninefreestyle.org
So you think you have a natural born Frisbee catcher? What better way to learn the newest tricks, enter contests, and win titles? Contact the WCFO to meet other Frisbee-playing dogs.

8. AMERICAN MIXED BREED OBEDIENCE REGISTRY

P.O. Box 7841
Rockford, IL 61126
www.amborUSA.org
The number one breed is . . . you guessed it, the mixed breed. So have a little fun with your dog. AMBOR has everything you want and need to enable your mixed breed to compete. Become a member, enter shows, send pictures, and meet all kinds of dog lovers.

9. ASSOCIATION OF PET DOG TRAINERS

66 Morris Avenue, Suite 2A
Springfield, NJ 07081
800-PET-DOGS
www.apdt.com
Ever dream of becoming a professional dog trainer? Learn from the best how to train your dog and become a trainer. This organization has a wonderful reputation for answering questions and solving common canine problems.

10. **THERAPY DOGS INTERNATIONAL**

88 Bartley Road
Flanders, NJ 07836
973-252-9800
www.tdi-dog.org
This volunteer group provides qualified handlers and
their therapy dogs for visits to institutions and facilities
where therapy dogs are needed. To learn more about
this great program (and how you can help), contact
Therapy Dogs International.

Top Dog Magazines

1. *Animal Fair*
   www.animalfair.com
2. *American Kennel Club Gazette*
   www.akc.org/pubs
3. *Clean Run Magazine*
   www.cleanrun.com
4. *Dogs in Canada*
   www.dogsincanada.com
5. *Dog Fancy*
   www.dogfancy.com
6. *Dogs Today*
   dogstoday@dial.pipex.com
7. *Dog World*
   www.dogworldmag.com
8. *Front and Finish*
   www.frontfinish.com
9. *Good Dog!*
   www.gooddogmagazine.com
10. *Your Dog*
    800-829-5116

Dog Web Sites

1. American Kennel Club
   www.akc.org
2. Bark
   www.thebark.com
3. The Dogpatch
   www.dogpatch.com
4. Dogwise
   www.dogwise.com
5. Gooddoggs.org
   www.gooddogz.org
6. The Kennel Club
   www.the-kennel-club.org.uk
7. The United Kennel Club
   www.ukcdogs.com
8. Hunting Retriever Club
   www.hrc-ukc.com
9. The Westminster Kennel Club
   www.westminsterkennelclub.org
10. Traveldog.com
    www.traveldog.com

Resources for Pet Supplies

1. Doctors Foster & Smith
   www.drsfostersmith.com
2. Red Dog Pet Supplies.com
   www.reddogpetsupplies.com
3. DOGtoys.COM
   www.dogtoys.com
4. J and J Supplies
   www.jjdog.com
5. KV Vet Supply
   www.kvvet.com
6. Dogwise
   www.dogwise.com
7. Cherrybrook
   www.cherrybrook.com
8. J-B Pet Supplies, Inc.
   www.jbpet.com
9. Petco.com
   www.petco.com
10. Petsmart
    www.petsmart.com

Top Spas for Dogs

With our hectic lifestyles, dog spas have become very popular, allowing our furry friends to frolic and play. Beyond the day care benefits, many of these spas offer therapy for injured animals. Training, grooming, boarding, veterinary care, and behavior consultation are all part of the package.

1. **DOG SPA**

145 West 18th Street
New York, NY 10011
or
32 West 25th Street
New York, NY 10010
212-243-1199
www.dogspa.com

2. **HAPPY TAILS DOG SPA**

8528-F Tyco Road
Tysons Corner, VA 22182
703-821-0700
www.happytailsdogspa.com

3. **ANIMAL FITNESS CENTER**

302 Blohm Avenue
Aromas, CA 95004
408-997-0828
www.dogtherapy.com

4. **SAVANNAH PET COMPLEX**

7203 Skidaway Road
Savannah, GA 31406
912-355-FETCH (3382)
www.petcomplex.com/hydro_dog.htm

5. **BEST FRIENDS PET RESORT AND SALON**

8224 Bash Street
Indianapolis, IN 46250
317-841-8182
www.bestfriendspetcare.com

6. **CAROLINA CANINE CENTER**

2104 Georgia Street
Greensboro, NC 27408
336-373-9663
www.carolinacanine.com

7. **PAWABILITIES, UNLIMITED**

1415 Liberty Street NE
Salem, OR 97303
(503) 399-1180
www.everythingpawsible.com (under construction)

8. **OLDE TOWNE PET RESORT**

8101 Alban Road
Springfield, VA 22150

703-455-9000
www.oldetownepetresort.com

9. THE DOGG HOUSE

2101 Berkmar Drive
Charlottesville, VA 22901
434-975-DOGS
www.thedogghouse.com

10. HALO HOUSE ANIMAL RESORT

3241 Delsea Drive
Franklinville, NJ 08322
856-694-0980
www.halohouseanimalresort.com

Can't Find a Location Near You?

The Pet Professor offers a guide for dog spas nearest you.
www.thepetprofessor.com

Looking for a great gift idea for your furry friend?
www.presents4pets.com

Do you want to open your own spa for dogs?
www.lapawspa.com.

notes

Top Dog Myths of Our Time

1. Cooper, Paulette, and Paul Noble. *277 Secrets Your Dog Wants You to Know*. Berkeley: Ten Speed Press, 1995, p. 65.

The Beginning of the Dog

1. Beauchamp, Richard. *Dog Breeding for Dummies*. New York: Hungry Minds, 2002, pp. 59–61.
2. Witz, A. "First Dogs in Asia." *Dallas Morning News* (November 22, 2003): 1A.
3. *Simon & Schuster's Guide to Dogs*. New York: Fireside Books, 1980, pp. 11–12

Famous Canines in History

1. www.bordeauxdogue.net/history.html.
2. Ibid.
3. www.takingthelead.co.uk.
4. Ibid.
5. *Simon & Schuster's Guide to Dogs*. New York: Fireside Books, 1980), p. 24.

6. www.sosstbernard.org/historydr.htm.
7. www.takingthelead.co.uk.
8. Ibid.

Dogs of Royalty

1. Dogs through History, www.cbc.ca/passiona-teeyesunday/feature_281203.html.

Modern-Day Classifications

1. Beauchamp, Richard. *Breeding for Dummies.* New York: Hungry Minds, 2002, pp. 68–69.
2. www.akc.org.

Dogs in Mythology

1. Bolton, Lesley. *The Everything Book of Classical Mythology.* Avon, MA: Adams Media, 2002.
2. www.nationmaster.com/encyclopedia/list-of-fictional-dogs.
3. www.campusprogram.com/reference/en/wikipedia/l/li/list_of_dieties.html.
4. Ibid.
5. www.indigogroup.co.uk/edge/bdogs.htm.
6. www.theoi.com/Ouranos/KuonKhrysseos.html.
7. Black Dogs in Mythology, www.indigogroup.co.uk/edge/bdogs/htm.
8. L'Estrange, Sir Roger, and Samuel Croxall. *The Fables of Aesop.* New York: Books, Inc., pp. 201–202; www.pitt.edu.

Canines and Proverbs

1. www.doghause.com/.

Evolution of the Canine

1. *Simon and Schuster's Guide to Dogs*. New York: Fireside Books, 1980, p. 12.

Canine Quotes

1. www.useful-information.info/quotations/dog_quotes.html.

Lucas and the Dogs of September 11th

1. ARDA. *Search and Rescue Dogs: Training the K-9 Hero*. New York: Howell Books, 2002, p. 1.
2. Ibid., pp.177–180.

Search and Rescue Dogs In Times of Disaster

1. ARDA. *Search and Rescue Dogs: Training the K-9 Hero*. New York: Howell Books, 2002, pp. 215–235.

Dogs in Prison

1. Wittenauger, Cheryl. "Missouri Inmates Train Dogs, Help Themselves." *Halifax Herald Limited* (December 30, 2000).

K-9s in Law Enforcement

1. "Top Dog Charlie Retires after a Career Sniffing Out Trouble." *USA Today* (September 24, 1999).

An Akita and the O. J. Simpson Case

1. Cooper, Paulette, and Paul Noble. *277 Secrets Your Dog Wants You to Know*. Berkeley: Ten Speed Press, 1995, p. 29.
2. Ibid., p. 31.
3. Ibid.

Everyday Dogs Turned Heroes

1. www.dogsinthenews.com/issues/0203/articles/020322a.htm.
2. www.ananova.com/news/story/sm_361838.html.
3. www.dogfancy.com/dogfancy.
4. Ibid.
5. www.takingthelead.co.uk.
6. "Dosha the Wonder Dog." *People Magazine* (May 12, 2003): 188.
7. *Dogs.* New York: DK Publishing Book, 1997, p. 118.
8. www.dogsinthenews.com/issues/0109/articles/010914a.htm.
9. "Faithful Dog Leads Blind Man 70 Floors Down." www.dogsinthenews.com, 11 (3) (September 14, 2001).

Best Barking Watchdogs

1. www.petrix.com/dogsec/topsec.html.

Breeds Least Likely to Succeed as Watchdogs

1. www.petrix.com/dogsec/topsec.html.

Most Popular Dog Names

1. www.petrix.com/dognames.

Most Famous Dogs of Our Time

1. www.citizenlunchbox.com/famous/animals.html.

How to Break Your Dog into Showbiz

1. www.hollywoodpaws.com.

First Dogs in the White House

1. www.presidentialpetmuseum.com.
2. Ibid.
3. Ibid.
4. www.lbjlib.utexas.edu.
5. www.presidentialpetmuseum.com.
6. www.ford.utexas.edu.
7. www.reagan.utexas.edu.
8. www.presidentialpetmuseum.com.
9. Ibid.
10. Ibid.

The Real Story about Dalmatians

1. Schlegl-Kofler, Katharina. *Dalmatians*. New York: Barron's, 1999, pp. 2–7.

William Wegman and His Weimaraners

1. Mudge, Allen. "When Is A Puppy Not A Puppy?" (November 15, 1997), www.bookpage.com.

Mush! Top Sled Dog Races of All Time

1. *Atta Girl! A Celebration of Women in Sport*. Terre Haute, IN: Wish Publications, 2003, pp. 65–66.

Index